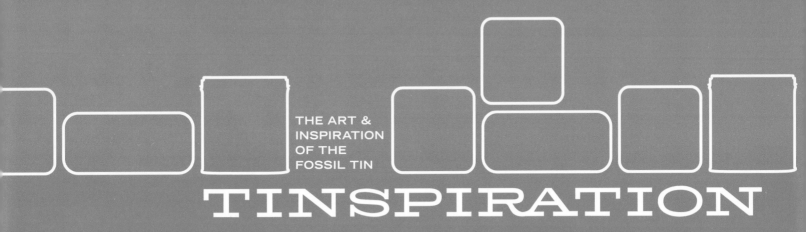

THE ART &
INSPIRATION
OF THE
FOSSIL TIN

TINSPIRATION

Contents

What if a package could communicate the soul of a brand?

What if the package served not simply as a container for products, but as a canvas for creativity? What if it could increase the perceived value of the product?

These are just a few of the questions the designers at Fossil entertained back in 1989 when they set out to design the packaging for their watches. They found their answers and their inspiration in something from the past, specifically, the colorful tin packaging of the 1940s and 50s. What resulted from this creative revelation was more than a container for the product. The Fossil watch tin expressed, in surprising fashion, the essence of a young, fun, authentic brand and the creative culture that spawned it. The concept altered the basic notion of the role that packaging played in the shopping experience. Like the cookie jar at your grandmother's house, these tins embodied a hidden emotional connection that added value to the product and the customer's experience with the brand. The philosophy Fossil adopted made the package a part of both the product itself and the total brand experience.

The tin has helped define
who Fossil is in a broad,
vintage, visual language.

Seventeen years and over 1,000 designs later, the concept remains fresh due to the company's ability to update the form and reinvent the graphic context the tins reflect. Fossil now produces over 7 million tins each year, each of them as eagerly sought after as the first ones made. These clever little boxes have worked their way into the fabric of customers' lives. You'll find them holding spare change on dresser tables, sugar packets in the kitchen, or secret mementos in the corner of a sock drawer. You can also find them traded on Ebay and sold at flea markets alongside the antiques that inspired them. And to this day, nothing conveys the creative soul of the Fossil brand quite like these iconic tin boxes.

From Fossil's perspective...
"VINTAGE IS EVERYTHING".

There is a certain richness to items that have weathered and grown in value with age. In that respect, Fossil has drawn on a wide variety of vintage sources for inspiration. Of course, the curious thing about the word "vintage" is that it means different things to different people and is constantly evolving. In the earliest days of the brand, there was an affinity for Americana imagery, the kind that expressed the sunny optimism of America in the late 40s & 50s.

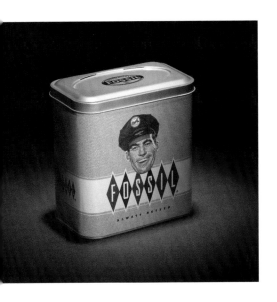

The tin box served as a natural extension of the earliest vintage-inspired watch designs, not only in form but also in its ability to deliver the authentic look and feel of the same period. Reference material for typography and graphic styling were readily available from packaging as diverse as oil cans, tobacco, consumer products and cosmetics. It gave a voice to the brand presentation with both a uniquely ironic wit and a differentiating graphic identity.

These days, the range of what is deemed "vintage" has a much broader interpretation. It includes references that predate the 50s, to more recent graphic inspiration from 60s and 70s rock & roll and blues, to the early video game graphics of the 80s. In all of these instances, the opportunity exists to interpret, romanticize, celebrate and update the emotional attachments and graphic styling of the tin to make them more relevant at any given time. In a way, Fossil's tin package has become a running dialogue with Fossil's customers. The tin inherently communicates those qualities that have helped the brand endure: inspired creativity, innovation and authenticity.

And, the original idea they hit upon so many years ago – the notion of a package that people would want to keep and treasure – still holds true today.

Oh yeah, it
does a pretty good
job of holding a
wrist watch too!

12

Hook your heels on a corral fence in Phoenix ...step out smartly at an Indiana barn dance...or wander through a cool forest in Maine. Wherever you do your playing, it's more fun in real Cowboy Boots. You get that wonderful "don't-fence-me-in" feeling every time you slip 'em on!

TESTED IN THE STIRRUP WHERE IT REALLY COUNTS

Take Me Out To

The Ballgame...

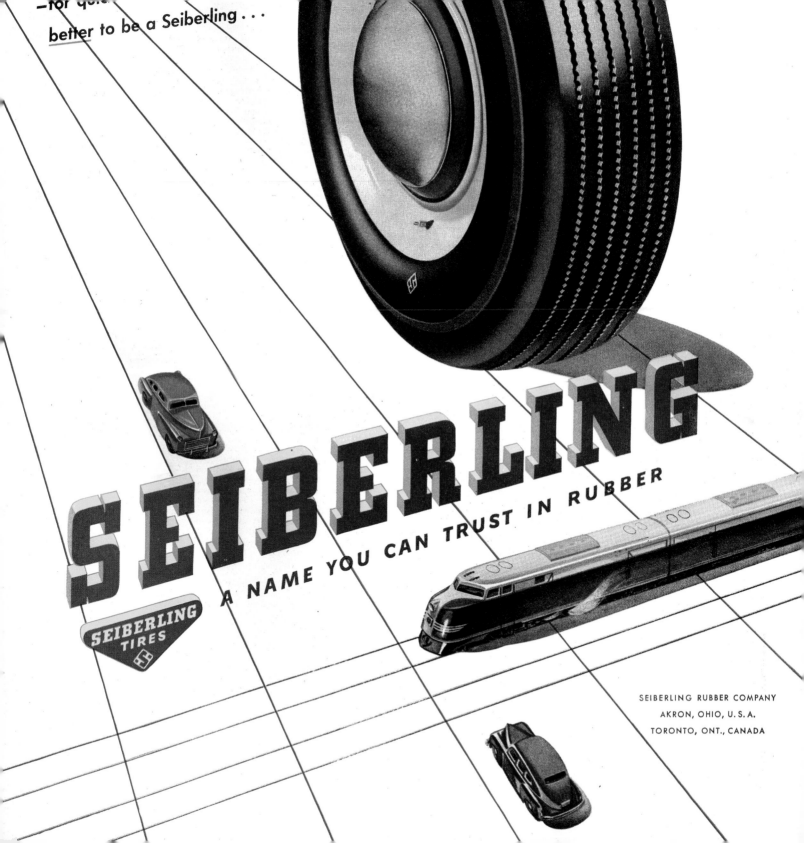

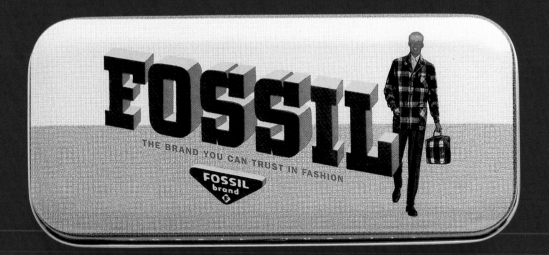

There's **One Sure Way**

to solve today's driving problems

McCall's

1956

**TEN HAIRDOS
THAT MAKE
FASHION NEWS!**

**TWO GREAT
PERSONAL**

quent hairdressers at all, but take care of their own hair. Whoever does it, a model's hair must be beautifully cared for. If it needs washing once a week, and most hair does, then that is what it should have. A mild alkali-free soap should be used, and the shampoo should be preceded by a brief, brisk massage with the fingertips to loosen the scalp. Begin the massage at the base of the neck by pressing with the thumbs into this area, keeping the fingers spread out over the top of the head. Massage upwa⟨...⟩ same time attempting to "lift" the scalp. Continue the massa⟨...⟩ entire head tingles. After washing, the hair should be thoro⟨...⟩ The regular use of a lemon juice rinse is excellent, but th⟨...⟩ lowed by another rinse in clear water.

Of course, the cardinal rule for beautiful, healthy ⟨...⟩ N⟨...⟩ else makes it so luxuriant and brings out ⟨...⟩ should be done every day. It pays t⟨...⟩ ⟨...⟩ to use it vigorously. Separate the ⟨...⟩ br⟨...⟩ well into the scalp at the beginning ⟨...⟩

Even the model who goes frequently to the ⟨...⟩ ⟨...⟩ her own hair in an emergency. She is o⟨...⟩ ⟨...⟩ure several times during a photographic sitting ⟨...⟩ ⟨...⟩ay, for example, be asked to wear it "up" with a ⟨...⟩ down when modeling sports things. She should wo⟨...⟩ hair arrangements that are smart and becoming and pr⟨...⟩ do them well and quickly. On page 50 you will find sk⟨...⟩ ⟨...⟩faces. These may be used as a ⟨...⟩ ⟨...⟩ is not intended that you slav⟨...⟩ ⟨...⟩ that you master the prin⟨...⟩ ⟨...⟩ the mode of the momen⟨...⟩ ⟨...⟩ coiffures each month. B⟨...⟩ ⟨...⟩ The crucial question is ⟨...⟩

Fossil
Classic

⟨...⟩ to prevent her pu⟨...⟩ ⟨...⟩gy of elegance whic⟨...⟩ ⟨...⟩t rings and she will ⟨...⟩ ⟨...⟩l are dark blue in colo⟨...⟩ and ⟨...⟩ Black enamel does al⟨...⟩ ⟨...⟩dency thing. Emeralds and other green stones, as well as all red stones⟨...⟩ to make the hand look red. Rings ⟨...⟩uld always be worn with discretion. A woman ⟨...⟩ay pile on as many bracelets as s⟨...⟩⟨...⟩s and the effect is apt to be good, but with rings, just a few should be⟨...⟩ ⟨...⟩se should be chosen for shape as well as color.

If the fingers are inclined t⟨...⟩ ⟨...⟩he tips, a rather large ring, square in shape, will offset their s⟨...⟩ ⟨...⟩ make the fingers look pointed in con-trast. If the upper joint of ⟨...⟩ ⟨...⟩long, a wide ring with a large square or oval stone will mitigate ⟨...⟩

Necklaces, too, do nice t⟨...⟩ ⟨...⟩r wearers. The three quarter ⟨...⟩gth neck-⟨...⟩e is the most generally ⟨...⟩pointed pendant hung on such a ⟨...⟩lace will ⟨...⟩ to offset a too-rou⟨...⟩ ⟨...⟩t necklaces are youthful and ⟨...⟩ming ⟨...⟩e. The dogcol⟨...⟩ ⟨...⟩ite prop when an effect of aris⟨...⟩ntic ⟨...⟩sought. A j⟨...⟩ ⟨...⟩ black velvet tied with a bow ⟨...⟩ o⟨...⟩ar ⟨...⟩ of coquetry, ⟨...⟩ ⟨...⟩e a bit "Houp! La! La!" Jewelry ⟨...⟩l t⟨...⟩ ⟨...⟩en for what it ⟨...⟩ YOU. You will wear so many jewe⟨...⟩rin⟨...⟩r ⟨...⟩el, that, whe⟨...⟩ ⟨...⟩come to choose your own trinkets, yo⟨...⟩t b⟨...⟩ ⟨...⟩with tried a⟨...⟩stworthy taste.

TEST QUESTIONS ON SCRIPT 1

1. Give five reasons for entering on a career of modeling ....
2. Name eight models who have become stars in Hollywood............ l
3. Name three well-known artists who married their models............ at
4. To succeed as a model need a girl be a great beauty?............... ore
5. Name four different types of modeling .... it
6. Tell briefly how a model should walk .... itne!
7. Describe an effective entrance .... ne!
8. What is meant by "brushing through"?......................... ge
                                                                  the

Fossil
A real eye opener!

round face

DIFFERENT TYPES of MODELING

camouflage

long, narrow face

⟨...⟩ rouge in a circular area at ⟨...⟩s demonstrated in the center ⟨...⟩n. Blend edges. Lips should ⟨...⟩er full, especially at the lowe⟨...⟩

PIVOT & POSE

⟨...⟩romine⟨...⟩ ⟨...⟩e some⟨...⟩ ⟨...⟩s...sh⟨...⟩ ⟨...⟩ine HALF PIVOT ⟨...⟩temples. ⟨...⟩up shou ⟨...⟩ POSE, and ⟨...⟩ide in order ⟨...⟩ may occupy a greater space, and tend ⟨...⟩ the apparent width of your face at ⟨...⟩

principles of RUNWAY and PLATFORM routines

Fashion shows are of so many different types and are held under
such a variety of conditions that the routine has to be flexible.
...memorize the Runway and Platform principles demonstrated
...with will be of invaluable aid under the most trying conditions.

Not ...phs, but by the react... an audience does she judge
her wor... inaudible sigh ...rance on the runway in the
glamour... the ...udible applause breaks
forth spor... ...me well. If chatter
among the ... ...not so good! That bit of
business...
front r...

Comp...
minute...

Model's
COURSE
platform instructions

...comes through the curtain. She takes two steps...
...and makes a complete turn adopting the Millinery...
...(head work, of course). Surveying the audience, she...
...e of the platform and goes down the stairs, using t...
...que previously described. As she takes a step with...
...aises the right hand ... and vice versa. On the floo...
...salon or restaurant, she adopts Room Center Techniqu...
... see illustration ... is the name given the routine of...
...forth to about four or five people at the same time....
...n in front of any one group, the model directs her...
...al to take in four or five more people, and proceed...
...d the semi-circle or square in which her audience...

Fantastic Fossil

Lady Fossil FACE POWDER — More than a pretty face!

List of Conte...

ENTRANCE   STAGE   EXIT

DOTTED LINE SHOWS PEBBLE

BUYERS

INSTRUCTIONAL
MODEL'S

...lpturing your hair ...

the oval face

BORDEAUX MIXTURE

Simple Scientific Strong

1/- PER BOX

THE PERFECT PICTURE HANGER

Wear-Ever
ALUMINUM CLEANSER
A POWDER

EBERHAR

SENTINEL
UTILITY
FIRST AID KI

CONTENTS: Adhesive Plasters 2 in x 1 yd.
Mercurochrome (H.W. & D.) 1 Dram
2 Individual Gauze and Absorbent Cotton
Compresses • ¾" Handy Bandages
DISTRIBUTED BY
FOREST CITY PRODUCTS
CLEVELAND, OHIO

STOP
CREAM
DEODORANT
by Sue-Pree

KEEPS POTS AND PANS
BRIGHT AND CLEAN

EASY TO USE

RODUCT OF THE MAKERS OF
"Wear-Ever" ALUMINUM
NET WEIGHT 12 OZ.

McNess
PURE GROUND

CINNAMON

3 OUNCES NET WEIGHT

PACKED BY
FURST-McNESS COMPANY
CHEMISTS AND
MANUFACTURING PHARMACISTS
FREEPORT,
ILLINOIS, U.S.A.

KNOX
U.S.P. PLAIN
SPARKLIN
N°
GELATI

THE HIGHEST
MADE UN
CHARL
GELATI
Johnstown,

CONTAINS
4 ENVELOPES
of gelatine — each
envelope enough for
six servings

NET WEIG
TRADE MARK

TECHNOLOGY
ng all things that are good.

The
DEPENDABLE WATCH
FOSSIL ®
GENUINE CLASSIC

AUTHENTIC
FOSSIL
established in 1984

FOSSIL ®
AUTHENTIC PRODUCT

− high powered   long life +
FOSSIL BRAND
Genuine
AUTHENTIC   FOSSIL   ORIGINAL

TY • QUALITY

L

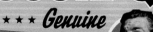

FOSSIL QUALITY
★★★ Genuine   Classic ★★★

FOSSIL ®

TRADE   MARK

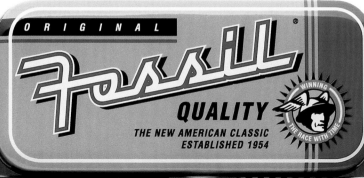

GENUINE
FOS
SIL
PRODUCTS
THE AMERICAN CLASSIC
1954
QUALITY
made with
PRIDE
CLASSIC
Consumers
Sold Coast

FOSSIL

Quality Crafted

DEVELOPED AND MA E ORIGINAL

ALWAYS CRAFTE

THE AMERICA ADE PRODUCTS

It

YOU KNOW

REGISTERED

TRADE MARK

JAPANESE
REFINED CAMPHOR

MANUFACTURED BY

THE NIPPON CAMPHOR CO LTD.,

KOBE JAPAN

original

classic

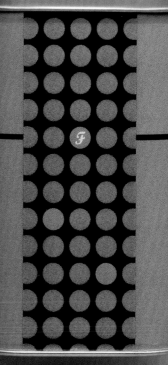

GEE'S LINCTUS PASTILLES
B.P.C.

CAUTION
It is dangerous to exceed the stated dose

ADULT DOSE
TO RELIEVE COUGH, DISSOLVE ONE
PASTILLE SLOWLY IN THE MOUTH

**NOT SUITABLE
FOR CHILDREN**

FOSSIL

AUTHENTIC

GENUINE CLASSIC

· 1954 ·

HE AMERICAN CLASS

ASTOR
GROUND

CLOVES

PACKED BY

ACM

for Accuracy

ADE IN   U.S.

LVE COR

MA

54

FOSSIL
BRAND

THE ORIGINAL AMERICAN CLASSIC
A RELIABLE AND ORIGINAL BRAND

SPECIALLY PREPARED FOR YOU

QUALITY & STYLE

FOSSIL

The American Classic

★ BRAND ★

OIOM

VAN DYKE

Density Graph

RHARD FA

TO OPEN PRESS HERE

St. Josep
ASPIRIN

NE DOZEN 5-GRAIN TABLE
GENUINE PURE ASPIRIN

A PRODUCT OF

Plough, Inc.

W YORK, N.Y. - MEMPHIS, TENN

10

A UNIQUE SELECTION OF

FOSSIL

UPERIOR QUALITIES SPECIALLY PREPARED
FOR YEAR ROUND ENJOYMENT

perior Quality

TRADE MARK

BOOK MATCHES

FEDERAL MATCHES

CLOSE COVER

HOM-OND Food Stores

SAN ANTONIO TEXAS

hotel BLACK

Oklahoma city.

DAN W. JAMES MGR.

COVER BEFORE STRIKING

POPULAR EVERYWHERE

FOSSIL GENUINE

FOSSIL

54 THE ORIGINAL Authentic BRAND

VANS REG. U.S. PAT. OFF.

LUXURY

WHITE FABRIC CLEANER

The Aristocrat of Shoe dressings

Manufactured by WILCO COMPANY Los Angeles, Calif.

SWELL FIT AND FORM

RCA RADIOTRON

RCA RCA

RADIO TUBE

SEALED and TESTED at the factory for YOUR PROTECTION

Kent DOUBLE EDGE · BLADES

De Luxe SPEEDWAY DOUBLE EDGE BLADES

54 GENUINE

Quality and Authentic Style

FOSSIL BRAND

POPULAR EVERYWHERE

THE
GENUINE
TRADE 54 MARK
POPULAR 54 EVERYWHERE
FOSSIL BRAND

Turmeric
Whole

Schiliing
SINCE 1881

2¼ OZS.

McCORMICK & CO., INC.
Baltimore   San Francisco   New York

The
Ben Milam
HOTEL
TEXAS AT CRAWFORD

provides
these services
CONVENIENCE

COFFEE SHOP
GARAGE

2000   No. 49
GENUINE
MAJOR Staples

PRECISION MADE

1954

(F)

Fossil

GENUINE
QUALITY

"Popular
Everywhere"

1954

AMERICAN
☆☆☆ BALL BLUE
WHITENS CLOTHES

G
54

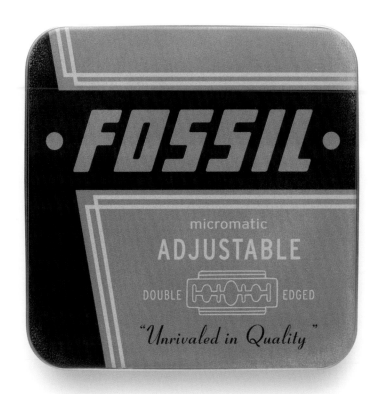

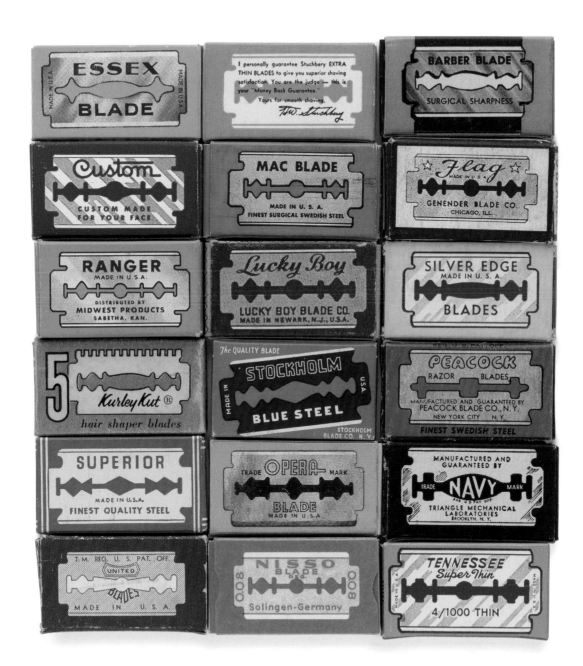

TISSUE THIN BLADES
FROM THE SOUTH'S STEEL CENTER

Sch... BLADE

DOUBLE EDGED

TOWN-TALK
DOUBLE EDGE
RAZOR BLADES

ALTO
NON TEMPERING
TOOL STEEL

SOS
SO SMOOTH
Double Edged
BLADES
Mfd. by SHEFFIELD MFG. CORP.
NEWARK, N. J.
Trade Marks Reg'd U. S. Pat. Off.

DUCKWALL
BLUE STEEL
DOUBLE EDGE
BLADES

DOUBLE EDGE
VULCAN
TRADE MARK
LEATHER STROPPED

Eliminate all Shaving Discomforts
'NDERES
Dependable
RAZOR BLADES
1

FOSSIL

DOUBLE EDGE
MEDIUM WEIGHT
"FOR NORMAL BEARDS"

blades by WREN

CITY
DOUBLE EDGE
RAZOR BLADES

Sheer
4/1000" THIN BLADES
HAIR SPRING STEEL

Climax
5 for 10¢
DOUBLE EDGE
BLADES

McNESS
Scotsman
DOUBLE EDGE BLADES

MACY'S
Double - Edge
SAFETY RAZOR
BLADES

FOSSIL

THIN

DOUBLE EDGED

NO: 54

EXTRA
SMOOTH

"The World's Closest Shave"

Extra Duty
DOUBLE EDGE
RAZOR BLADES
FOR EXTRA SHAVES

America's Most
Magnificent Bourb
OLD
HICKOR

AJAX
DOUBLE EDGE
BLUED
SWEDISH
STEEL

TATRA

Genuine
CORONA
TRADE MARK   REG. U.S. PAT. OFF.
DOUBLE EDGE
RAZOR BLADES

FLUID DRIVE FOR
A SMOOTH RIDE
DOD

Ever-Ready

CORUX
double edge

ELGIN
REG. U.S. PAT. OFF.
THE PRECISION
BLADE

AMOLA BLADE FOR
A SMOOTH SHAVE
AMO
STE

ATLAS

CONTINENTAL
REG. U. S. PAT. OFF.

Eastmor
TRADE MARK

5 TWENTY 10

Watertow
THE PERFECT BLAD

FOSSIL Fresh
Laundry Powder
LEAVES CLOTHES WITH OUTDOOR FRESHNESS!

FOSSIL'S Bravo
Dish Soap
CONCENTRATED LOW SUDS
Easy on hands!

PROFESSIONAL PROSHINE
LIQUID CAR WASH
FOSSIL INSTITUTE OF TECHNOLOGY

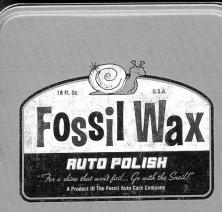

18 Fl. Oz.   U.S.A.
Fossil Wax
AUTO POLISH
"For a shine that won't fail... Go with the Snail!"
A Product Of The Fossil Auto Care Company

Fossil Magic
HOUSEHOLD CLEANER
Dirt and grime disappear instantly!

New!
FOSSIL honey
MAKES EVERYTHING TASTE BETTER...

Fossil
FOAMING ACTION
WOW CLEANSER
TOUGH ENOUGH FOR YOUR KIDS WORST SPILLS!

FOSSIL
BIG BULL
FOAMING ACTION UPHOLSTERY CLEANER
FOSSIL CLEANING COMPANY • ESTABLISHED 1954

FOSSIL
SUD-Z
BUBBLE BATH
Will not irritate eyes

take five

george cates

AUTHENTIC
ORIGINAL
GENUINE
FOS
SIL!
AUTHENTIC

1954
THE AMERICAN CLASSIC

FOSSIL
THE AMERICAN CLASSIC

SBT0220 12/99

GENUINE AUTHENTIC ORIGINAL
GENUINE
FOSSIL
BRAND
THE AMERICAN CLASSIC 1954

ORIGINAL
1954
FOSSIL
THE AMERICAN CLASSIC

yes indeed!

ATLANTIC 802

les charles

FULL *dynamics-frequency* SPECTRUM

FOSSIL 1954

Worth a
thousand
words

under some available light conditions a picture may result where the subject is too dark. the use of the flash the picture tremendously under these conditions. when t upon subject brightness the shutter speed second or even slower in the bulb mode.

FOSSIL 1954
Bring on the road for in the pavement
lies promise

Classic

are you free this weekend   what is your sign   what time do you have   friday

thinking
of the right
words to say

do you like the movies   may i have your number   that sounds great

FOSSIL 1954

FOSSIL 1954   The New
American
Classic

54

INSIST ON THIS BRAND

TRADE **FOSSIL** MARK

FOR QUALITY AND VALUE

FOR QUALITY
and VALUE
CHOOSE

QUALITY
PRODUCTS
SINCE 1954

FOSSIL

U.S.A.

1954

THE ORIGINAL AMERICAN CLASSIC
A RELIABLE AND ORIGINAL BRAND

54

FOSSIL

CLASSIC AMERICAN BRAND

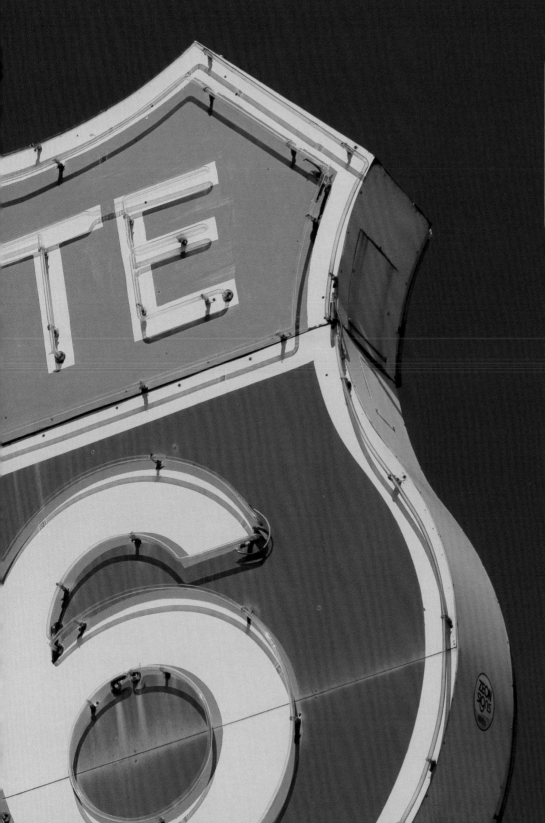

The Roosevelt
The Pride of the South
New Orleans
PALMOLIVE

Aotel
Warden
Fort Dodge
Iowa

HENR
PAL
ATL

BERG

MEYER HOTELS
The Windsor
JACKSONVILLE, FLA.
The Roosevelt
JACKSONVILLE, FLA.
The Floridan
JACKSONVILLE, FLA.
The Farragut
KNOXVILLE, TENN.
The Hermitage
NASHVILLE, TENN.
The Sir Walter
RALEIGH, N.C.
The Patrick Henry
ROANOKE, VA.
The Emerson
BALTIMORE, MD.
FINER HOTELS

Whitley
HOTEL
MONTGOMERY'S LARGEST
Mark L. Grable, Mgr.

THE *Albert Pike*
HOTEL
LITTLE ROCK, ARK.

TEL
LA.

Rice Hotel
Houston

the
ORANGE BLOSSOM
hotel
SARASOTA, FLORIDA

BENTLEY HO
ALEXANDRIA,

SCHIMMEL
"HOST TO THE MOST"

HOTEL
HILLSBORO
TAMPA, FLORIDA

HUCKINS
Hotel
BROADWAY AT MAIN
OKLAHOMA CITY, OKLAHOMA

MEYER H

BH

Boss Hotels
EDWIN A. BOSS
President

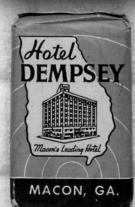

Hotel
DEMPSEY
Macon's Leading Hotel
MACON, GA.

El Comodoro Hotel
S W FIRST STREET AT SECOND AVENUE
Miami, Florida

FINER HO

MAKE MORE SALES WITH
MATCH BOOK ADVERTISING

PEOPLE DO READ

MATCH BOOK
ADVERTISING

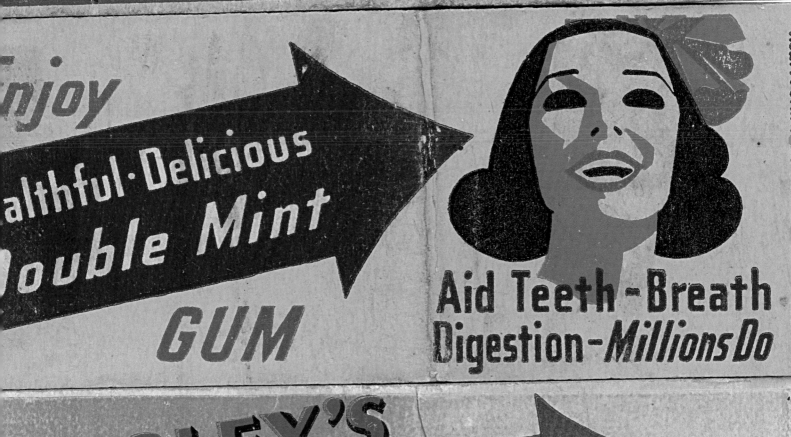

Look for GENUINE FOSSIL PRODUCTS *wherever THEY'RE SOLD*

THE
FOSSIL
BRAND

1954 ORIGINAL GENUINE

THE AMERICAN CLASSIC

ROUTE OF
The Streamliners

DIRECT
FOSSIL
LINE

Low Fares EVERYWHERE EVERY DAY

DOUBLE EDGE

20 for 25¢

Marlin

THE MARLIN FIREARMS CO
NEW HAVEN CONN

Marlin

15 for 25¢

SINGLE EDGE

for

SPARK PLUGS

CHAMPION

Dependable

CHAMPIONS USE CHAMPIONS

THE PERFECTLY BALANCED MOTOR OIL

CITIES SERVICE
MOTOR OIL

CITIES SERVICE

At All
College Stations

Built for Southern Roads

ACME TIRES

ACME CO.

REM

REL

for head colds

Built for Southern Roads

FOSSIL

ACME CO.
6.50-18

**GUARANTEED AGAINST
ALL ROAD HAZARDS**

FOSSIL BRAND CO.
NEW AND IMPROVED

Fossil
20 to 25¢

AUTHENTIC

THE FOX RIG AND

ERATING SINCE 1915

THE FOX RIG AND LUMBER CO.

1101 Franklin St.

WHITE TRUCK SALES & SERVICE COMPANY

TRUCKS AND BUSSES

White's

ROUTE OF *The Streamliners*

CHICAGO AND NORTH WESTERN LINE

ROUTE OF THE FAMOUS **400**

Low Fares EVERYWHERE EVERY DAY

Try Us For

GUARANTY BARBER SHOP

505 ELM ST.
Phone - 372

GOOD APPEARAN
A WISE INVESTMEN

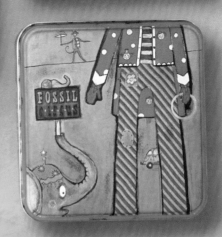

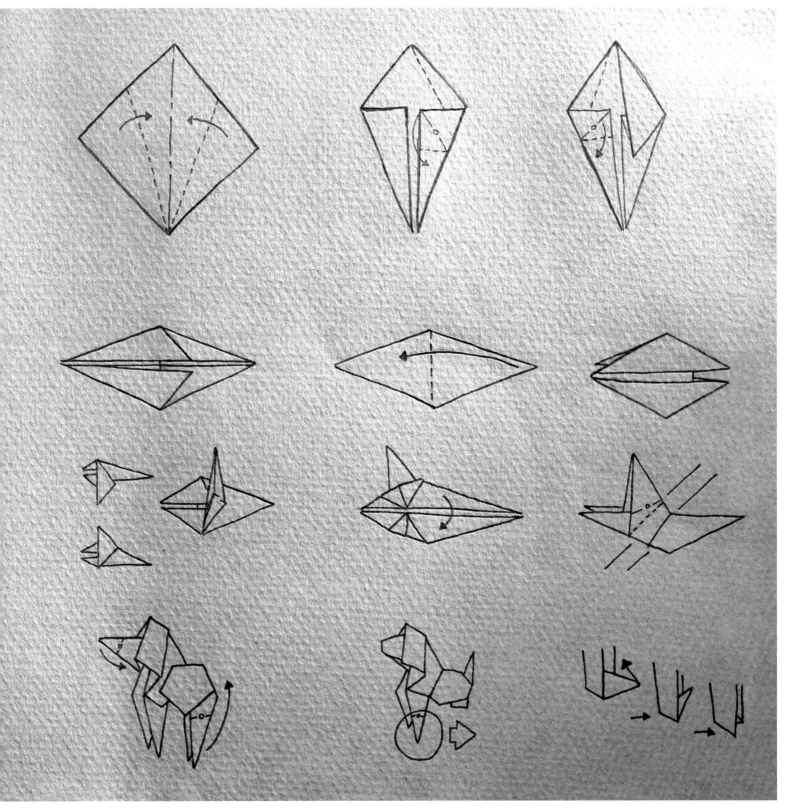

BASIC STITCHES

RANDOM CROSS STITCH

SATIN S

PADDED SATIN

RUNNING STITCH

OUTLINE FILLING STITCH

4 3 2 1
IN OUT IN OUT

BULLION STITCH

LONG & SHO

WHIPPED RUNNING STITCH

WHIPPE

CROSS STITCH

DARNING STITCH

BACK STITCH

STRAIGHT STITCH

1 OUT   3 OUT

2 IN   4 IN

FRENCH KNOT FILLING STITCH

GERMAN KNOT STITCH

MACRAMÉ STITCH

1 2
OUT IN

1 OUT
2 IN

2 IN 4 IN

1 3 5
OUT OUT

4 IN   OUT

2 IN   OUT

BUTTONHOLE STITCH

2 IN 4 IN 6 IN

OUT 3   5
OUT   OUT
1
OUT

BUTTONHOLE FILLING STITCH

MARSTON.
a 1825 - Lima
Peru. S.A.

FOSSIL
E. 2ND ST.

U.S. FOSSIL 3¢
IN GOD WE TRUST

My Dad's older
brother—mining
engineer

FOSSIL WILDLIFE DIVISION

FOSSIL NATURE CLUB

FOSSIL FISHING ASSOCIATION

FOSSIL BOTANICAL SOCIETY

School is good.
It's good to be good.

GOOD CITIZENSHIP
IN THE
COMMUNITY

GOOD
CITIZENSHIP
STARTS WITH
YOU

A GOOD
CITIZEN
IS SAFE

GOOD
CITIZENSHIP
IN THE
FAMILY

...SVILLE

...FORNIA

CHICO

CALIFORNIA

© CURT TEICH & CO., INC. 3B-H1699

3B-H414

RICH...

Vi...

Greetings from

BUQUERQUE

NEW MEXICO

A-26

D-7

Howdy from

DALLAS

TEXAS

© CURT TEICH & CO., INC. 2B-H628

VF-64

Greeting

From

FO...

© C. T. & CO.

...KA

2B-H309

Greetings from

OSHKOSH

WISCONSIN

© CURT TEICH & CO., INC. 1B-H2478

Greetings from

MONTE...

CA...

© CURT TEICH & CO., INC.

V67

GREETINGS

from

L19

Greetings from

FORT

WORTH

Greetin...

FRO...

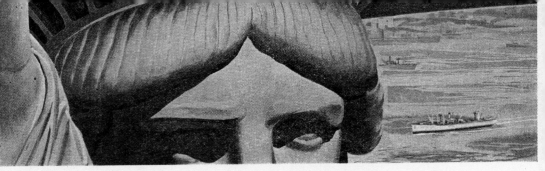

xplore the National Parks, drive through Yellowstone, osemite and Sequoia. (Please do not feed the bears.)

Wave to the ships of foreign lands from Liberty's mighty crown. (In New York — so many things to see.) From coast to coast, it's a land filled with sights that delight the whole family. Discover America this summer.

when you stop at the *Happy Motoring* sign

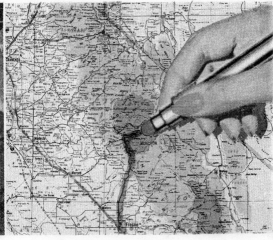

atch for this sign as you drive. Coast to coast, it's r assurance of regularly-inspected, clean restrooms . . .

plenty of towels . . . a sparkling mirror . . . you'll find this cleanliness a comfort, especially with children.

Fossil's famous Touring Service will plot your trip on America's most popular road maps. Ask your Fossil dealer.

Make America's First Choice yours, too!

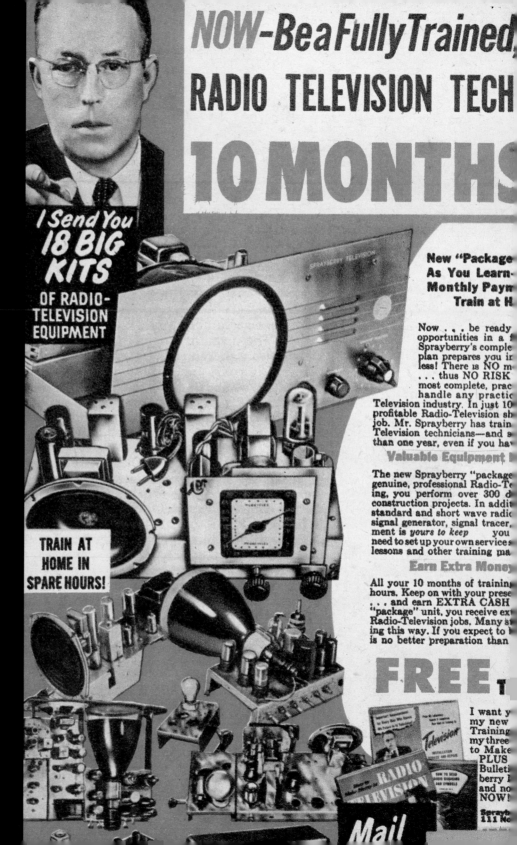

hi-fi

fossil

ELECTRIC POWERED FOR MODERN PEOPLE!

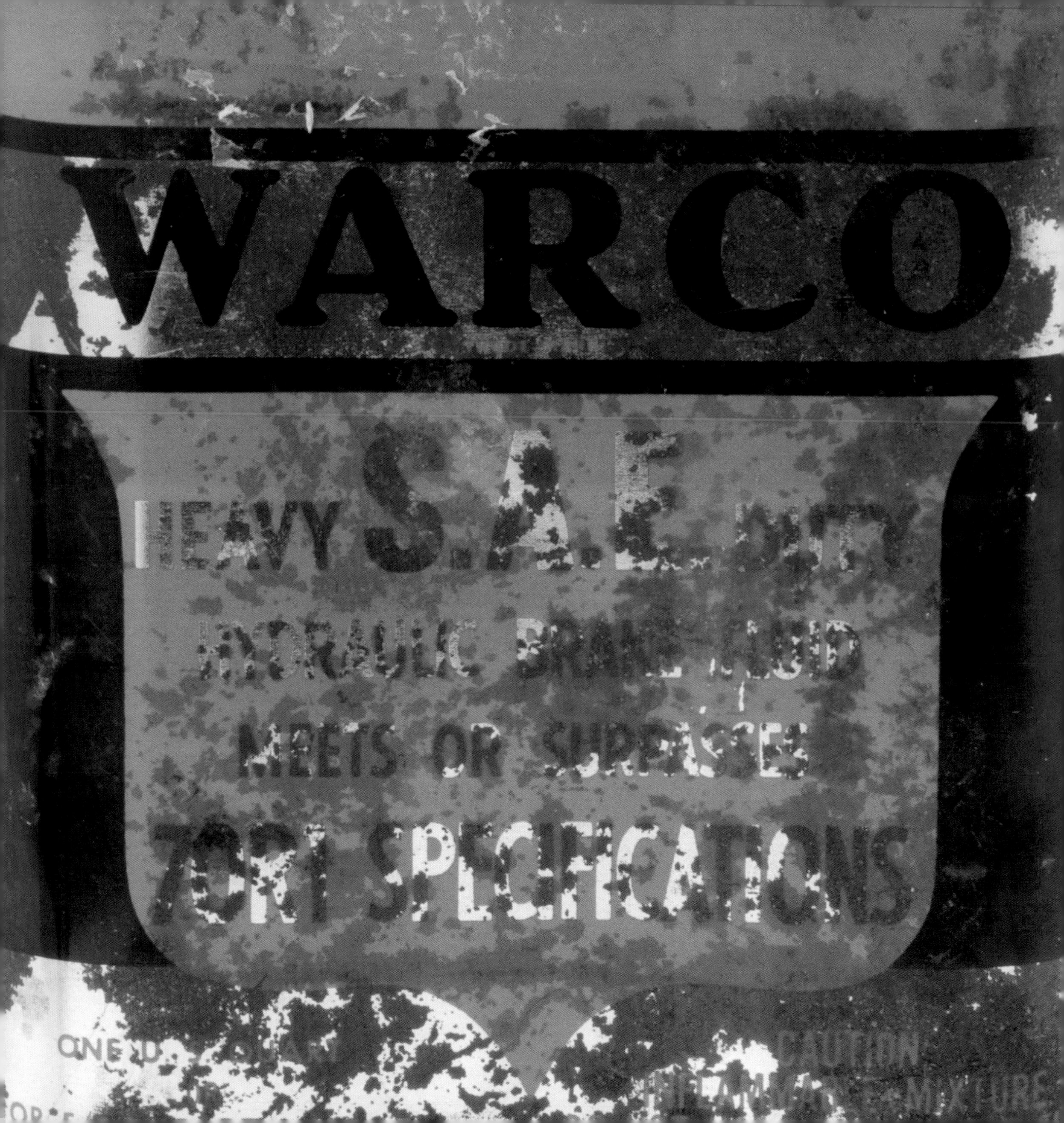

WARCO

HEAVY **S.A.E.** DUTY
HYDRAULIC BRAKE FLUID
MEETS OR SURPASSES
TORI SPECIFICATIONS

ONE ... CAUTION
FLAMMABLE MIXTURE

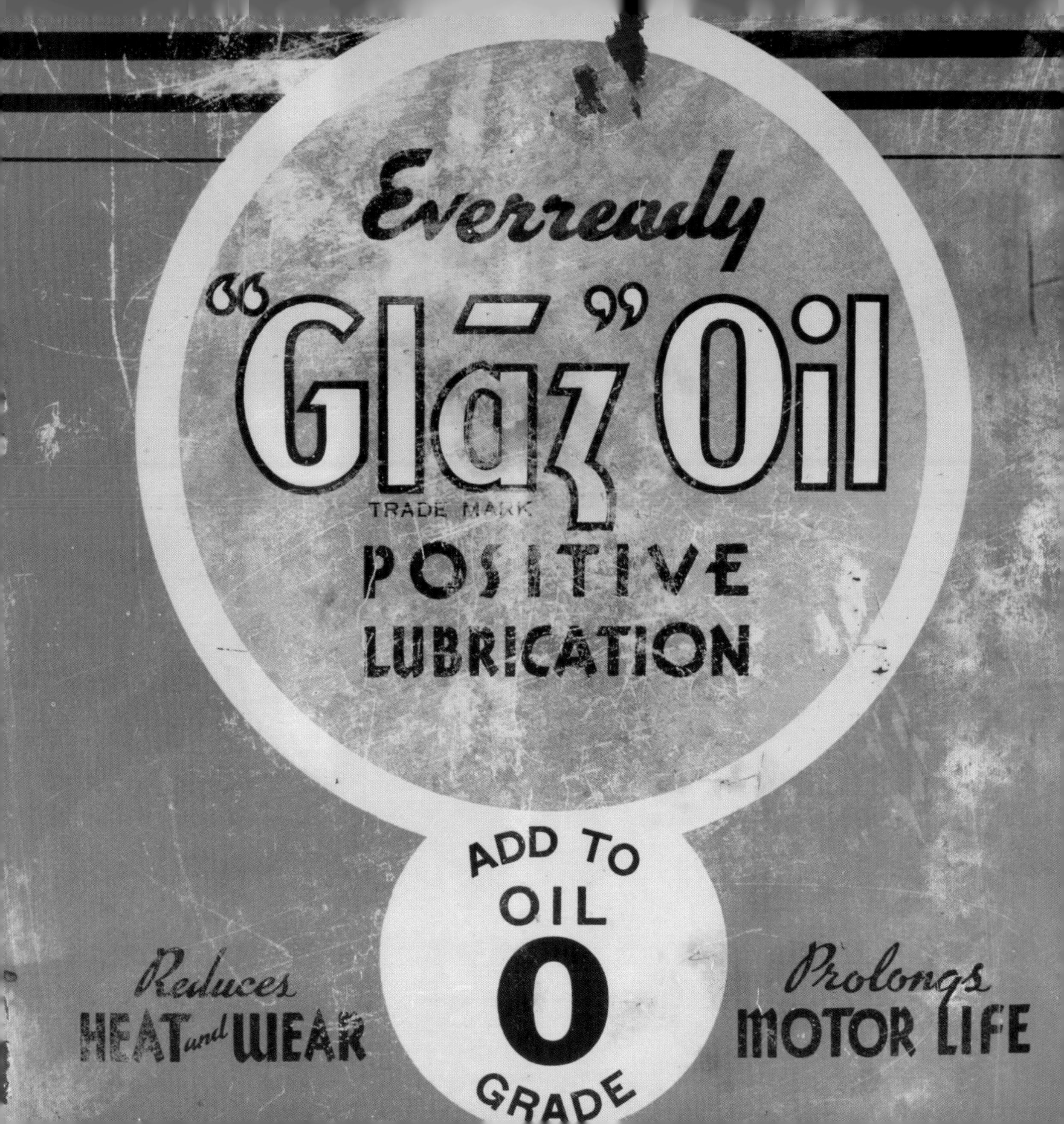
Eveready
"Glāz" Oil
TRADE MARK
POSITIVE
LUBRICATION
ADD TO
OIL
O
GRADE
Reduces
HEAT and WEAR
Prolongs
MOTOR LIFE

FALCON
MOTOR OIL
ONE U.S. QUART

Durable *Tenacious*

OSCAR BRYANT
HOLLIS, OKLAHOMA

TOURING

RPM
SPECIAL
MOTOR OIL
NET. .946 LITRO NETO · 33 IMP. OZ.

THE NEW
PREMIUM-GRADE
FOR BETTER
PERFORMANCE
FOSSIL

FOSSIL
Refinery Sealed
MOTOR
WATCH
Performance Engineered
"FOR PEP AND POWER"
THE FOSSIL WATCH CO.

FOSSIL
WORLD'S FINEST
Quality 100%
SETTING THE STANDARD

SKELLY
Skelly Supreme
MOTOR OIL
EASIER STARTING
LOW CONSUMPTION
CLEANER MOTOR
SKELLY OIL COMPANY

FO
MO
WA
SETTING
THE FO

ONE

NO. 085
MARVEL
AIR-TOOL OIL
LUBRICATES AND PROTECTS
REMOVES GUMMY DEPOSITS
DANGER: COMBUSTIBLE
HARMFUL OR ... IF SWALLOWED
Se ... cautions on back.
NET 32 FL. OZ. (1 QUART)
.946 LITER — .833 IMP. QT.

FOSSIL
Refinery Sealed
MULTI-GRADE
Performance Engineered
"FOR PEP AND POWER"
THE FOSSIL MOTOR CO.

ROYAL
MOTOR OIL
FOR SERVICE ML

AT LOWER COST

...NAL REFINING CO.

SUPERIOR
F
FOSSIL
ALL-SEASON PROTECTION

Protecto
BRAND
...FROM HIGHEST QUALITY
...TO MEET THE LUBRICATION
...KINDS OF TODAY'S AUTOMOBILES
...AND INDUSTRIAL MACHINERY
GREASE
PETROLEUM CHEMICALS CO.

ALL PURPOSE
THE NEW
PREMIUM GRADE
TELLING TIME
IN STYLE
FOSSIL
ONE WATCH
FOSSIL WATCH CO.

PREMIUM
FOSSIL
QUALITY
Lasts Longer
SUPERIOR PERFORMANCE

HAVOLINE
MOTOR OIL
TEXACO
ONE U.S. QUART   0.946 LITRE

CUS
HA
MO
KEEPS

...R CRAFT

...RTS
fad

and ROADSTER CAVALCADE

ROD &
Custom
Frank

with AIR
SUSPENSION

MARCH 1957
25c

15×36

THUNDER ROD Details on page 12
from Utah

HB994

RODD'N
and *Re-styli...*

DECEMBER 25c

DOUG'S GREEN FROG — The Cha...

- refinish right!
PAINT LIKE THE EXPERTS
- seldom seen Sally
NEW TWIN GRILLE SWAP
- on-the-spot report
NHRA WORLD SERIES

YOUR AD
SEE "SWAP &

SPECIAL SECTION Power from Multi-Carb M...

R CRAFT

...S —'49 —'51 Ford Customs

AUGUST 1957 25c

...our Ca...

BARRIS SHOWS **7** TOP **NEW** STYLING IDEAS

First Issue!

Custom
Rodder

The Best Rod
For Under $300

•

FACELIFT
for '49 FORD
fast • easy • cheap

MAY ACE 25c

FRANK

15×64

SUPERCHARGED DEUCE
A Real Stormer!

How You Can Install

FRANK

DECEMB...

custom
cars

206
TAI
FO
'5

CUSTOM IDEAS for '55—'56—'57 CHEV...

Custom

PICTORIAL REPORT—Continental Kit St...

Custom

EDSE

OCTOBER 1957

25c

Fossil
CHOP SHOP

CHOPPED, PAINTED & SOLD ALL UNDER 24 HOURS

CAN'T FIND US? CALL 1-810-901-RODS FOR THE NEWEST LOCATION.

Red's
FULL SERVICE
FOSSIL SERVICE STATION

AMAZING
FOSSIL POWERED

EST. 1984

RACING CAMS

PUT MORE STING IN THE RING!

MILLER-GULF

SPECIFICATIONS

Power Unit .... In-line six
Valve Arrangement .... dohc, 2 valves per cylinder
Bore & Stroke .... 2.5 x 2.125 in (63.5 x 79.4mm)
Bore/Stroke ratio .... 8.85 to one
Displacement .... 180.4 cu in (2955cc)
Compression Ratio .... 5.46/1, 6.14/1 for Bonneville
Carburetion .... Dual downdraft supercharger, double-entry
                              Dual downdraft carbs, centrifugal supercharger (running
                              at 4.87 times engine speed)
Max. Power .... 246 bhp @ 6400 rpm
Final drive ratio .... 3.35 (Bonneville), 3.91, 3.57, 4.66
Wheelbase .... 108 in
Tread .... 57.4 in
Suspension .... Independent-unequal length wish-
                              bones and quarter-elliptic trans-
                              verse springs, and Hartford friction
                              type, per wheel. Houdaille hydraulic type
Shock absorbers .... Miller disc
Brakes .... 366 sq in
Brake lining area .... 6.50 x 18 and 7.00 x 18
Tire size .... Kelsey-Hayes, 70-spoke knock-off
Wheels .... 45.0 in
Length .... 2155 lb
Height 3.13
Weight .... 354 up in
Bhp per cu in .... 1730 fpm
Bhp per sq in piston area ....
Seconds per bhp .... 22.3 with 3.39 gears
Feet per min at max power ....

C.O. LaTourette

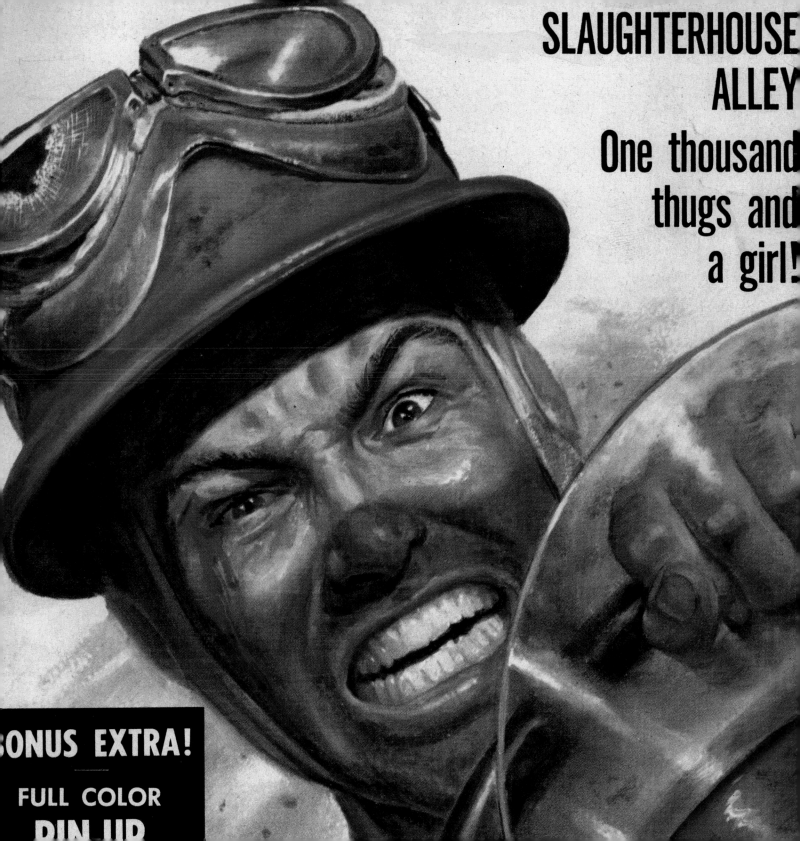

SLAUGHTERHOUSE
ALLEY
One thousand
thugs and
a girl!

BONUS EXTRA!

FULL COLOR
PIN-UP

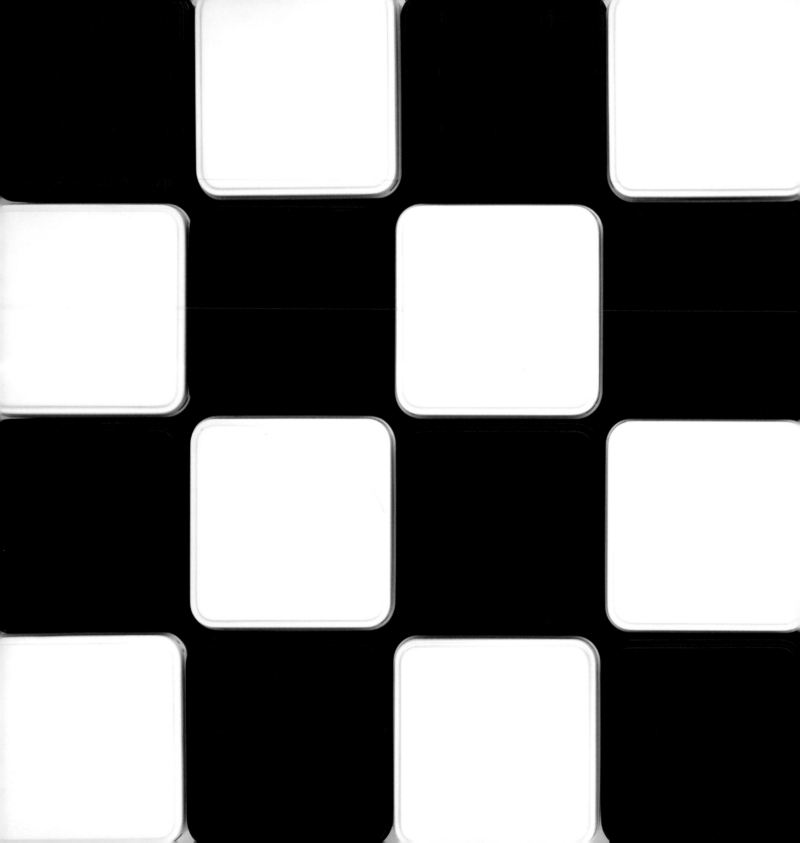

I'M WATCHING YOU

FOSSIL

FOSSIL

I SEE YOU

I'M WATCHING YOU

SSHHHH...

WHICH WAY DID THEY GO??

FOSSIL

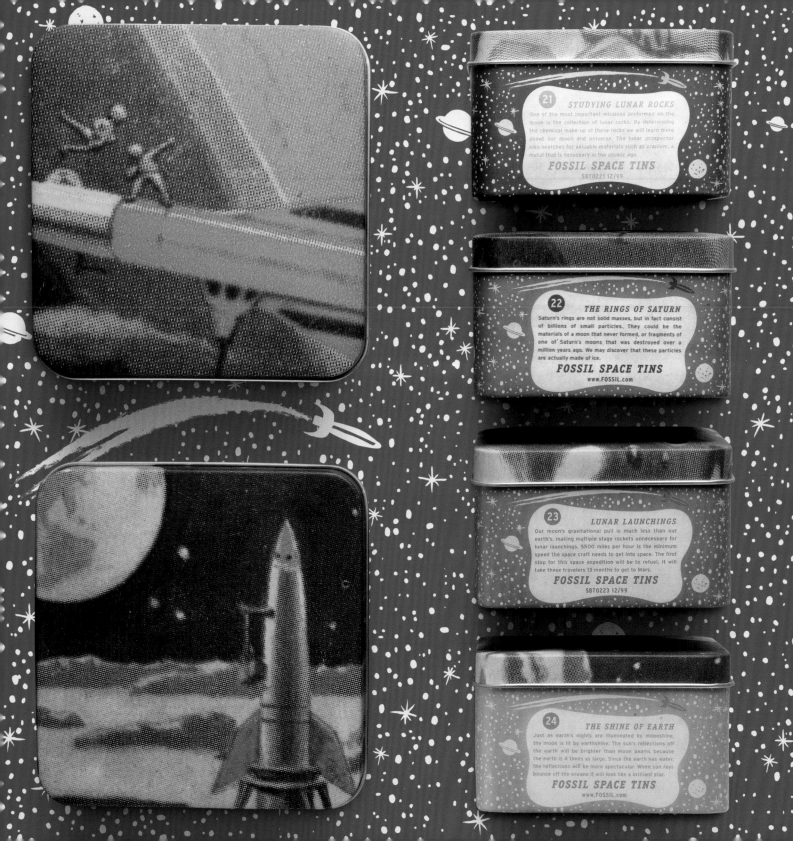

STUDYING LUNAR ROCKS

One of the most important missions preformed on the moon is the collection of lunar rocks. By determining the chemical make-up of these rocks we will learn more about our moon and universe. The lunar prospector also searches for valuable materials such as uranium, a metal that is necessary in the atomic age.

FOSSIL SPACE TINS

SBT0221 12/99

THE RINGS OF SATURN

Saturn's rings are not solid masses, but in fact consist of billions of small particles. They could be the materials of a moon that never formed, or fragments of one of Saturn's moons that was destroyed over a million years ago. We may discover that these particles are actually made of ice.

FOSSIL SPACE TINS

www.FOSSIL.com

LUNAR LAUNCHINGS

Our moon's gravitational pull is much less than our earth's, making multiple stage rockets unnecessary for lunar launchings. 5500 miles per hour is the minimum speed the space craft needs to get into space. The first stop for this space expedition will be to refuel, it will take these travelers 13 months to get to Mars.

FOSSIL SPACE TINS

SBT0223 12/99

THE SHINE OF EARTH

Just as earth's nights are illuminated by moonshine, the moon is lit by earthshine. The sun's reflections off the earth will be brighter than moon beams because the earth is 4 times as large. Since the earth has water, the reflections will be more spectacular. When sun rays bounce off the oceans it will look like a brilliant star.

FOSSIL SPACE TINS

www.FOSSIL.com

**Light-Propelled Space Ship
See Page 64**

15ᶜ

OCTOBER

See Page 10

**HAND - SCULPT
CLAY MODEL**

**TIN GRID FROM TOOL
FOR GRAPHICS PLOTTING**

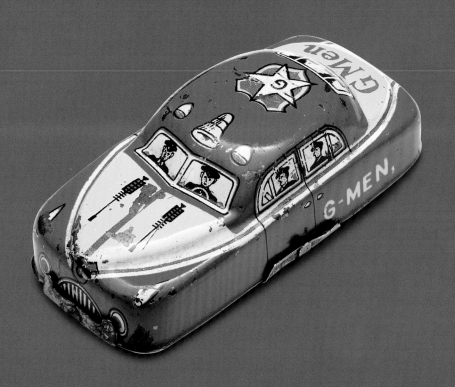

MADE EASY

A complete home instruction course in the Fox Trot — with two 45-rpm extended play records, illustrations and foot patterns.

17

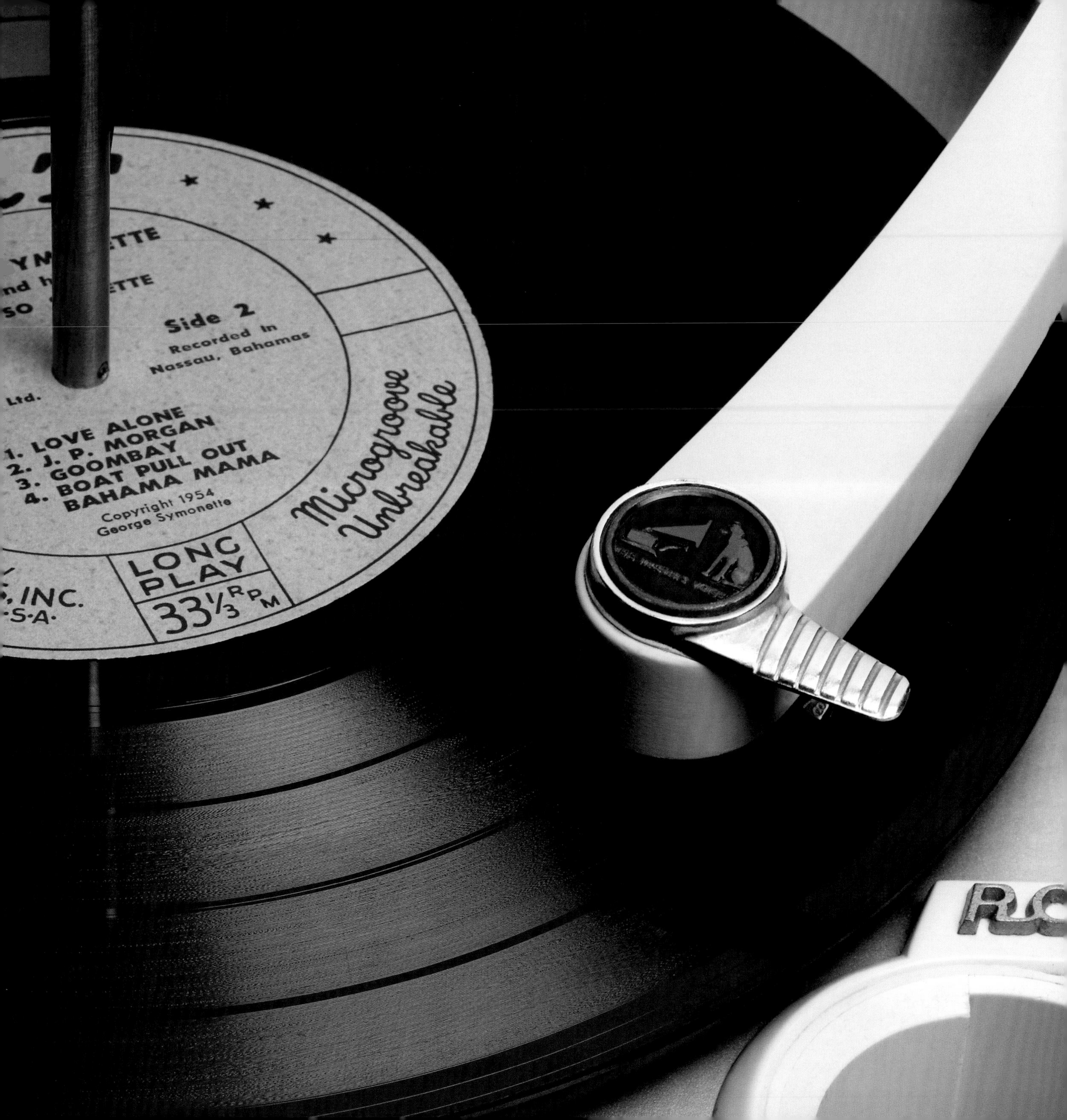

Side 2

Recorded in
Nassau, Bahamas

1. LOVE ALONE
2. J. P. MORGAN
3. GOOMBAY
4. BOAT PULL OUT
   BAHAMA MAMA

Copyright 1954
George Symonette

Microgroove
Unbreakable

LONG
PLAY
33⅓ RPM

LAISSEZ LES BON TEMP ROULEZ

RECORDS

MISTAKE • I'LL GET BY • JUST FOR A THRILL

Fossil

An American Original

classic

The New American Classic

FOSSIL

FOSSIL
MICROGROOVE

Genuine
Authentic
Original

FOSSIL *Classic*

fossil lp series 0055

STEREO

authenti

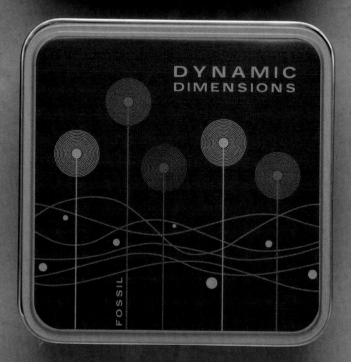

COLUMBIA

presents

DON BAKER

Organ Music

AT THE PARAMOUNT ORGAN   SET C-92

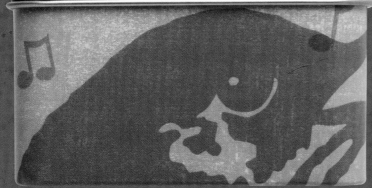

BROOKLYN ARENA
PRESENTS
FOSSIL ROCK

FOSSIL
ROCK

FOSSIL ROCK
★ ★ ★ presents ★ ★ ★
SOUTHERN SHOWCASE
RECORDED LIVE AT
The Grain Belt
volume no 2

FOSSIL

Fossil Rock
Truckstop Romance

Fossil Rock

FOSSIL ROCK
PRESENTS
southern showcase
RECORDED LIVE
AT
★ WILDCAT'S ★
volume no.1

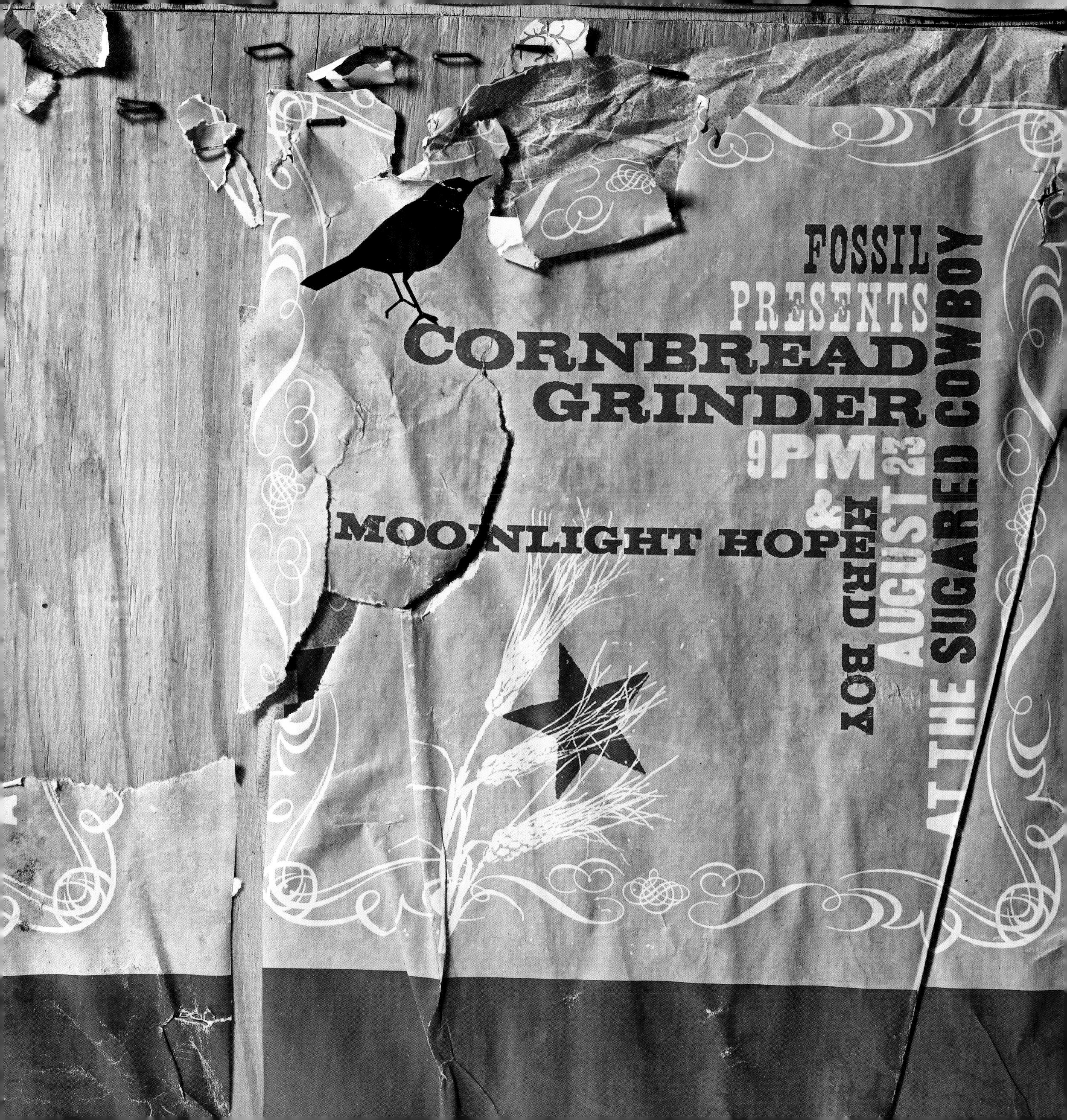

FOSSIL
PRESENTS
CORNBREAD
GRINDER
9PM
&
MOONLIGHT HOPE

HERD BOY

AUGUST 23

AT THE SUGARED COWBOY

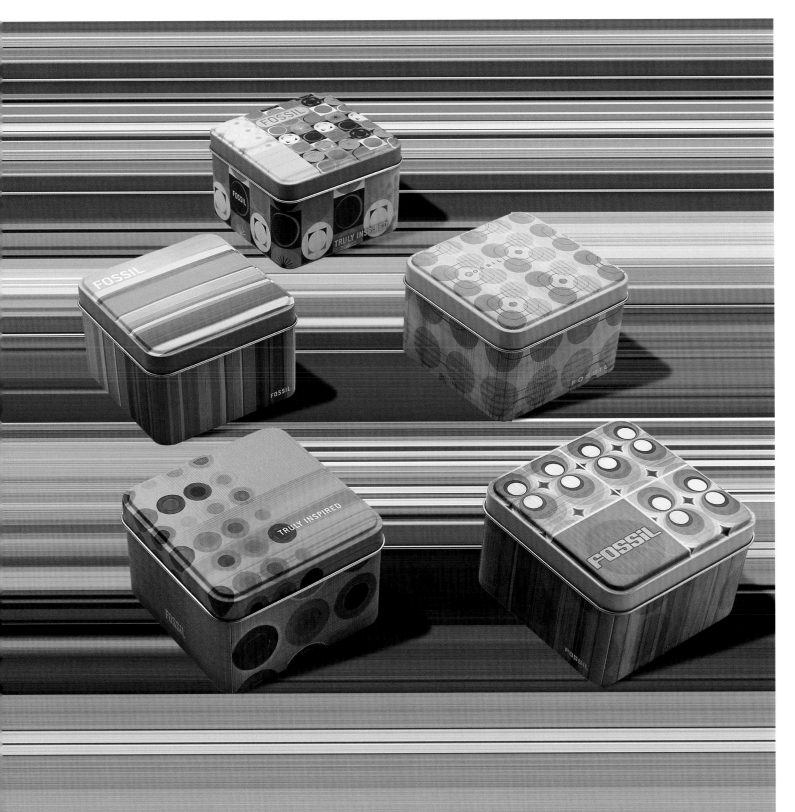

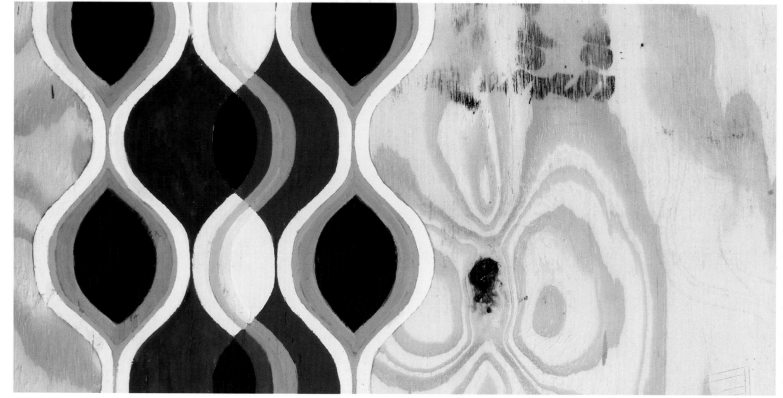

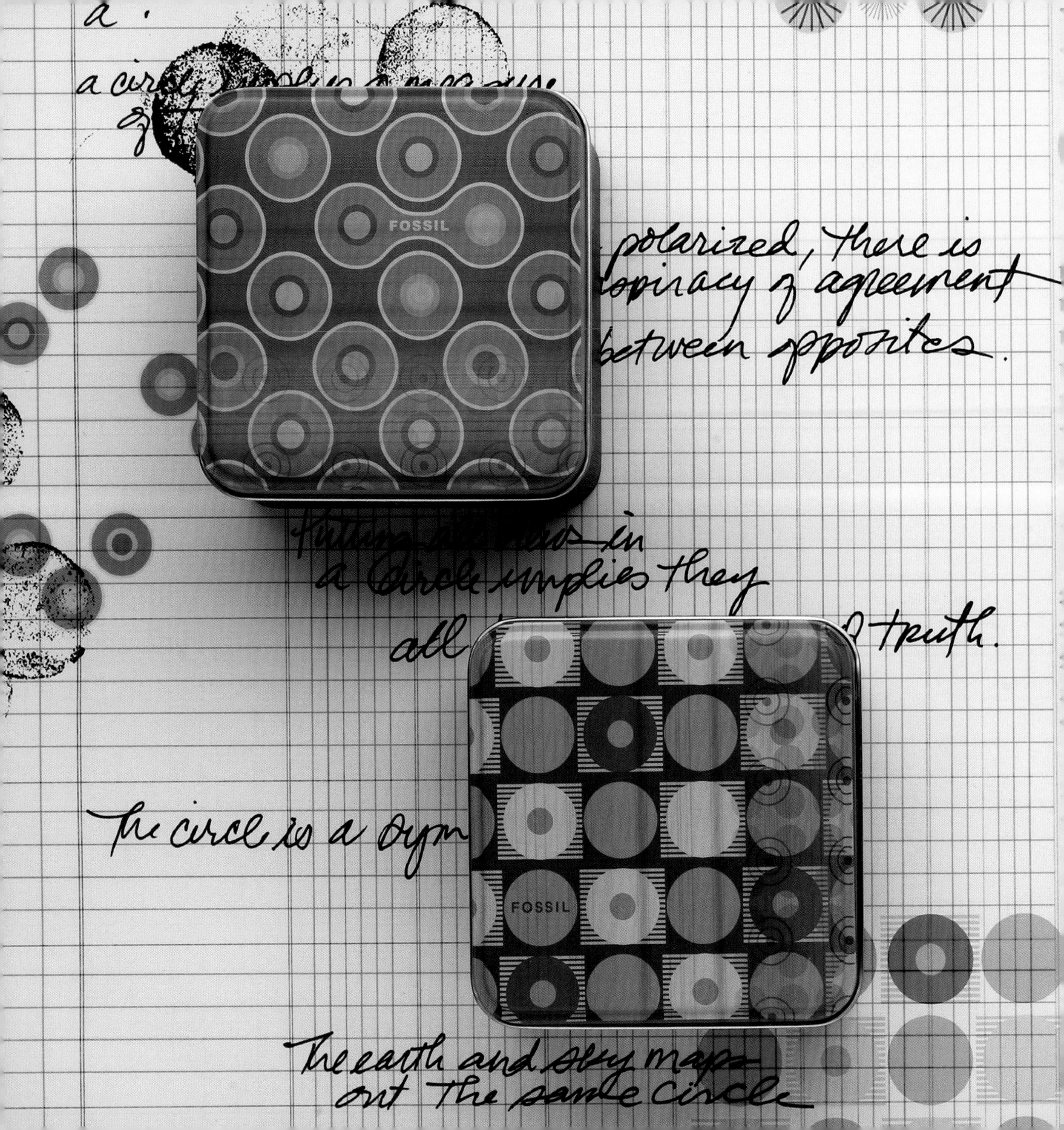

a .

a circle

polarized, there is
ovinacy of agreement
between opposites.

Putting ideas in
a circle implies they
all   truth.

The circle is a sym

The earth and sky maps
out the same circle

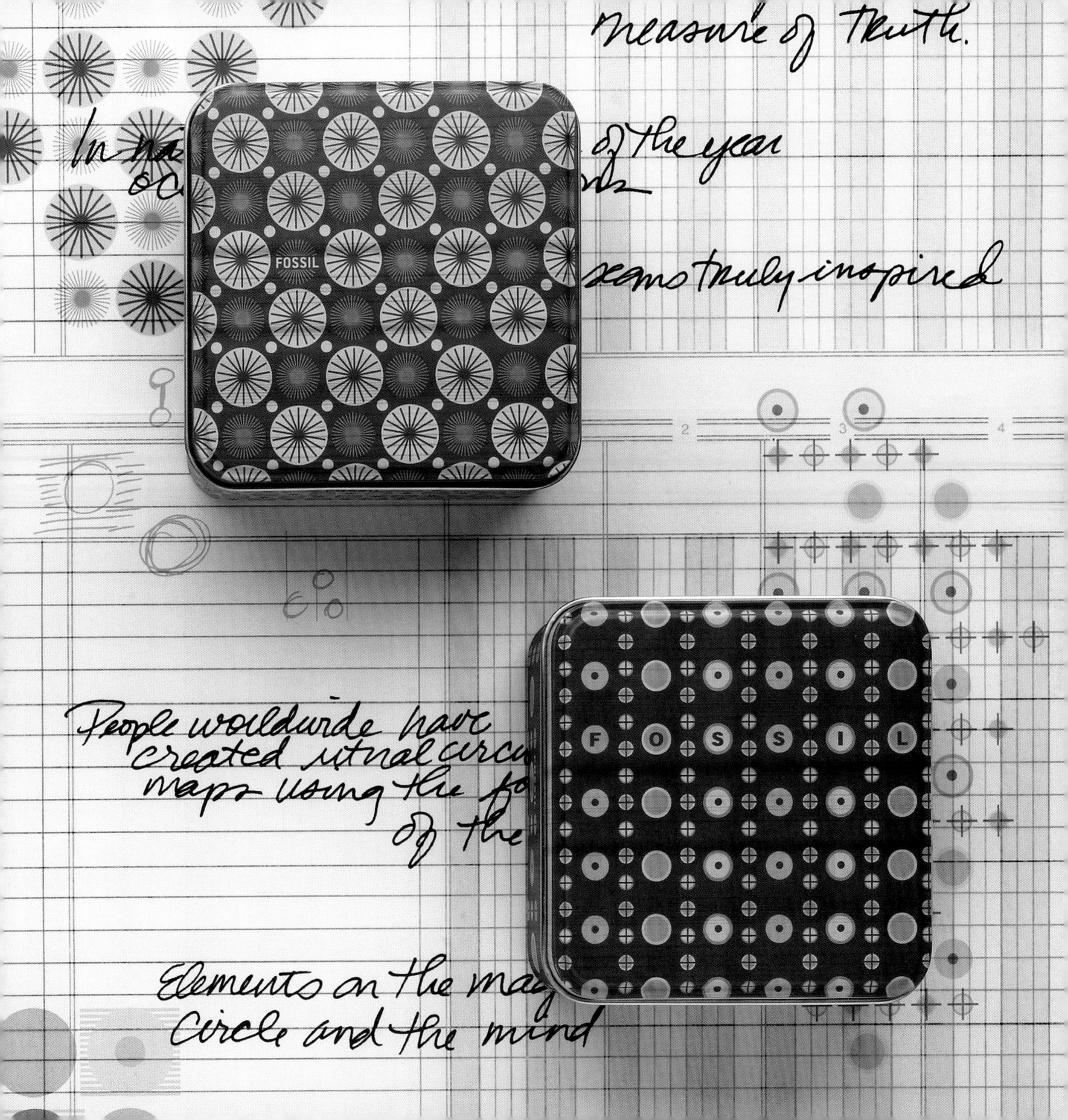

measure of truth.

In na... of the year

...seems truly inspired

FOSSIL

People worldwide have
created ritual circ...
maps using the fo...
of the

FOSSIL

Elements on the ma...
Circle and the mind

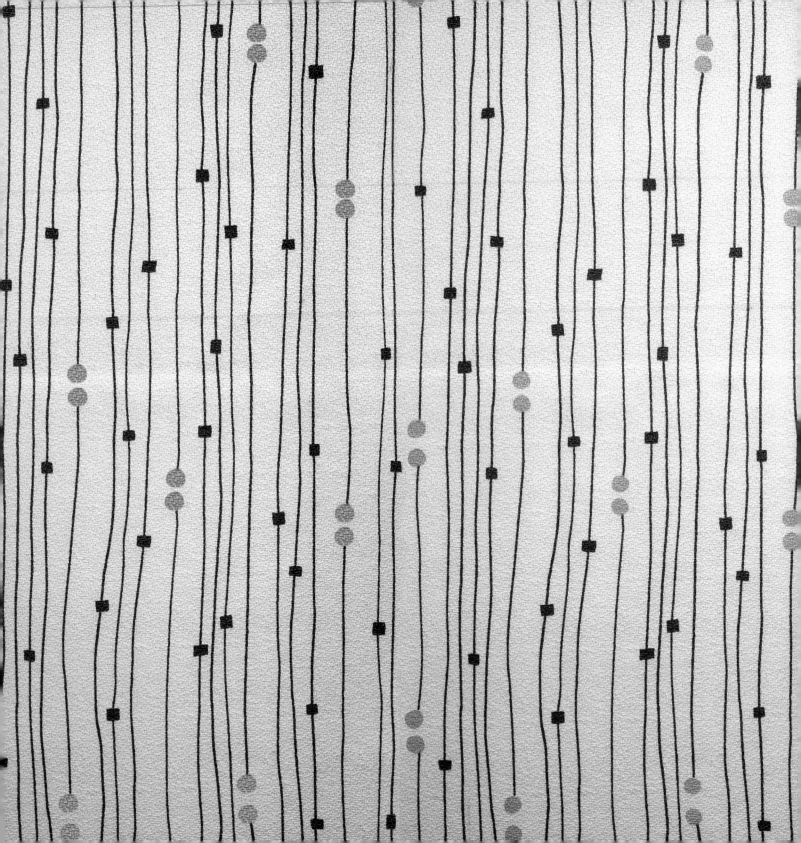

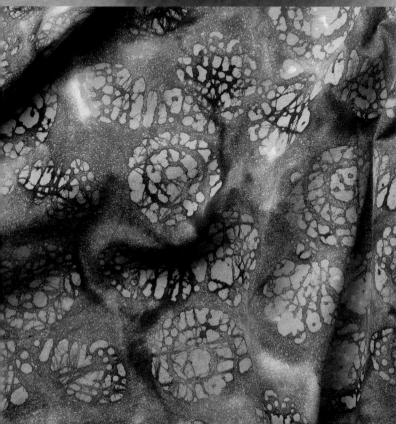

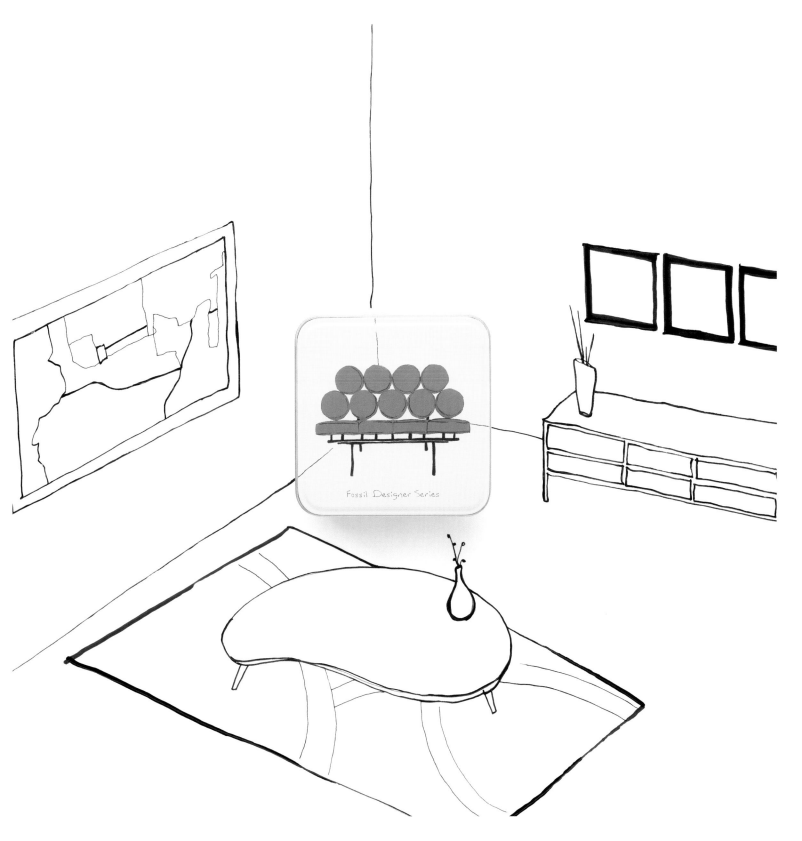

Fossil Designer Series

Special "New Idea" Items to add new interest to your home!

ADD-ON UNITS with the built-in look.

COCKTAIL TABLE with three "stowaway" TV snack tables.

BRUNCH TABLE with inset mar-resistant black plastic serving surface.

WALL VANITY WITH MIRROR and bench cushioned in foam rubber.

PANEL BED with adjustable-angle headboard for reading-in-bed comfort.

TEA CART, fully lined with mar-resistant plastic interior.

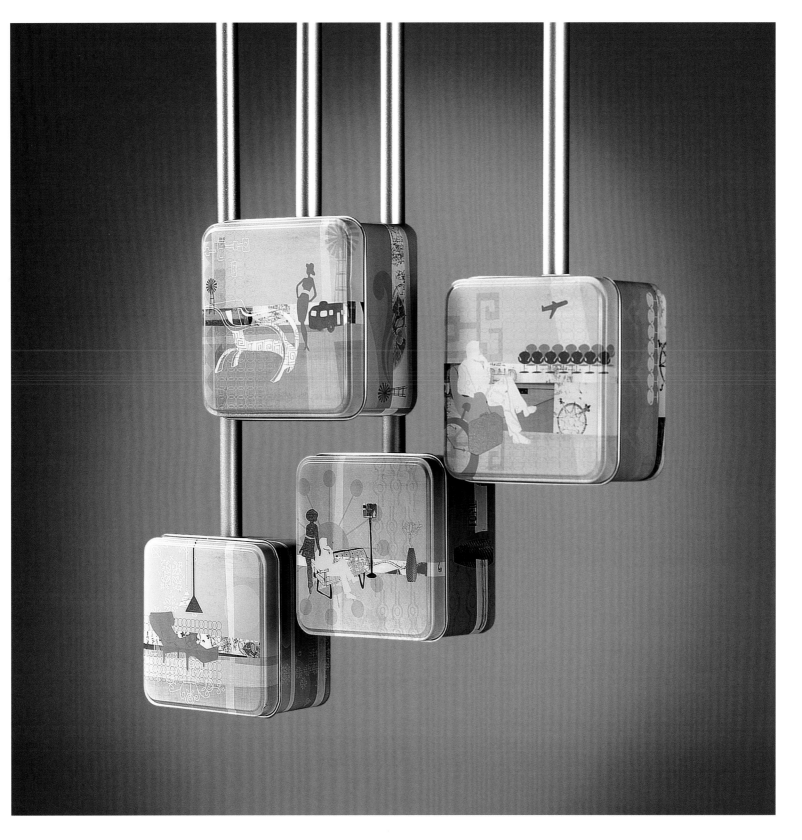

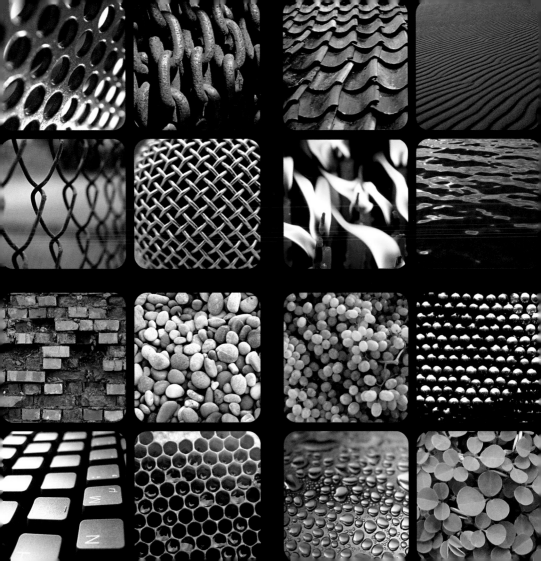

Tinology

0001A	0001B	0001C	0001D	0002A	0002B	0002C
0002D	0003A	0003B	0003C	0003D	0004A	0004B
0004C	0004D	0005A	0005B	0005C	0005D	0006A
0006B	0006C	0006D	0007A	0007B	0007C	0007D
0012A	0012B	0012C	0012D	0013C	0013D	0014A
0014B	0014C	0014D	0015A	0015B	0015C	0015D
0016A	0016B	0016C	0016D	0017A	0017B	0017C
0017D	0018A	0018B	0018C	0018D	0019A	0019B
0019C	0019D	0020A	0020B	0020C	0020D	0021A

0021B 0021C 0021D 0022A 0022B 0022C 0022D

0022E 0023A 0023B 0023C 0023D 0024A 0024B

0024C 0024D 0025A 0025B 0025C 0025D 0026A

0026B 0026C 0026D 0027A 0027B 0027C 0027D

0027E 0028A 0028B 0028C 0028D 0028E 0028F

0029A 0029B 0029C 0029D 0029E 0030A 0030B

0030C 0030D 0030E 0031A 0031B 0031C 0031D

0031E 0032A 0032B 0032C 0032D 0033A 0033B

0033C 0033D 0033E 0034A 0034B 0034C 0034D

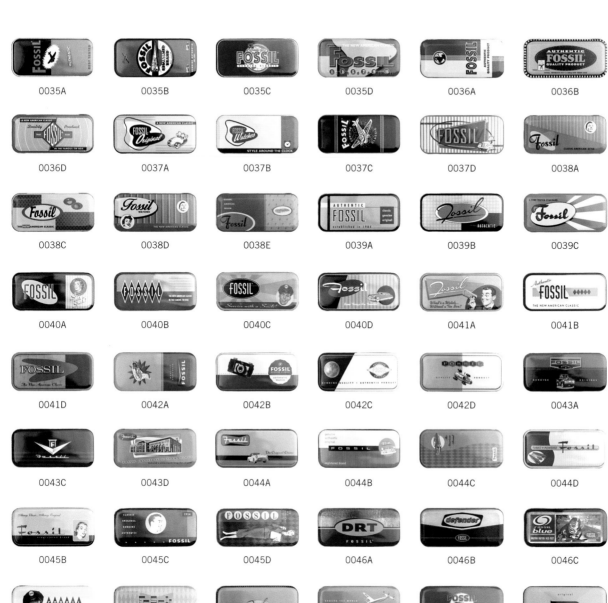

0035A 0035B 0035C 0035D 0036A 0036B 0036C

0036D 0037A 0037B 0037C 0037D 0038A 0038B

0038C 0038D 0038E 0039A 0039B 0039C 0039D

0040A 0040B 0040C 0040D 0041A 0041B 0041C

0041D 0042A 0042B 0042C 0042D 0043A 0043B

0043C 0043D 0044A 0044B 0044C 0044D 0045A

0045B 0045C 0045D 0046A 0046B 0046C 0046D

0047A 0047B 0047C 0047D 0048A 0048B 0048C

0048D 0049A 0049B 0049C 0049D 0050A 0050B

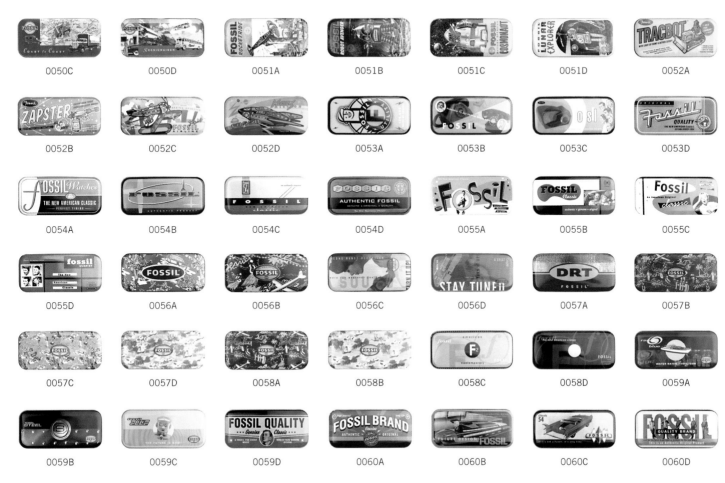

0050C

0050D

0051A

0051B

0051C

0051D

0052A

0052B

0052C

0052D

0053A

0053B

0053C

0053D

0054A

0054B

0054C

0054D

0055A

0055B

0055C

0055D

0056A

0056B

0056C

0056D

0057A

0057B

0057C

0057D

0058A

0058B

0058C

0058D

0059A

0059B

0059C

0059D

0060A

0060B

0060C

0060D

0060E

In 1996, it became apparent that the flat, rectangular form factor that was designed specifically for use with the original leather banded watches of the Fossil collection was becoming obsolete. This was due to a change in fashion trends and a move to watches with metal bracelets. In order to address the change in the market it was necessary to adopt a form factor that could package both the leather strapped watches and the emerging metal bracelet counterpart. The change allowed for more graphic presence due to the increased surface area and also enhanced the tin's ability to be used as a display accessory at the point of purchase.

BRC0001   BRC0002   BRC0003   BRC0004   BRC0005   BRC0006   BRC0007

BRC0008   BRC0009   BRC0010   BRC0011   BRC0012   BRC0013   BRC0014

BRC0015   BRC0016   BRC0017   BRC0018   BRC0019   BRC0020   BRC0022

BRC0023   BRC0024   BRC0026   BRC0027   BRC0028   BRC0029   BRC0031

BRC0032   BRC0034   BRC0037   BRC0038   BRC0039   BRC0040   BRC0041

BRC0042   BRC0043   BRC0044   BRC0045   BRC0047   BRC0049   BRC0050

BRC0051   BRC0052   BRC0053   BRC0054   BRC0055   BRC0056   BRC0057

BRC0058 BRC0059 BRC0060 BRC0061 BRC0062 BRC0063 BRC0064

BRC0065 BRC0066 BRC0067 BRC0068 BRC0069 BRC0070 BRC0071

BRC0072 BRC0073 BRC0074 BRC0075 BRC0076 BRC0077 BRC0079

BRC0080 BRC0081 BRC0082 BRC0083 BRC0084 BRC0085 BRC0086

BRC0087 BRC0088 BRC0089 BRC0090 BRC0091 BRC0092 BRC0093

BRC0094 BRC0095 BRC0096 BRC0097 BRC0098 BRC0099 BRC0100

BRC0101 BRC0102 BRC0103 BRC0104 BRC0105 BRC0106 BRC0107

BRC0108 BRC0109 BRC0110 BRC0111 BRC0112 BRC0113 BRC0114

BRC0115 BRC0116 BRC0117 BRC0118 BRC0119 BRC0120 BRC0121

BRC0122 BRC0123 BRC0125 BRC0126 BRC0127 BRC0128 BRC0130

BRC0132 BRC0133 BRC0134 BRC0135 BRC0136 BRC0137 BRC0138

BRC0139 BRC0140 BRC0141 BRC0142 BRC0143 BRC0144 BRC0145

BRC0146 BRC0147 BRC0148 BRC0149 BRC0150 BRC0151 BRC0152

BRC0153 BRC0154 BRC0155 BRC0156 BRC0157 BRC0158 BRC0159

BRC0160 BRC0161 BRC0163 BRC0164 BRC0165 BRC0166 BRC0167

BRC0170 BRC0171 BRC0172 BRC0173 BRC0175 BRC0176 BRC0177

BRC0178 BRC0179 BRC0180 BRC0181 BRC0182 BRC0183 BRC0184

BRC0185 BRC0186 BRC0188 BRC0189 BRC0190 BRC0191 BRC0192

BRC0193 BRC0194 BRC0195 BRC0196 BRC0197 BRC0198 BRC0199

BRC0200 BRC0201 BRC0202 BRC0203

In 1999, it was the consensus among the brand leadership and design staff that the bracelet tin needed to be updated to a different shape. The dimensions were still relevant for the product so it was decided to use a design that used approximately the same dimensions but took cues from the original flat tin design which utilized the lid more for graphic presentation.

SBT0205   SBT0206   SBT0207   SBT0208   SBT0209   SBT0210   SBT0211   SBT0212

SBT0213   SBT0214   SBT0215   SBT0216   SBT0217   SBT0218   SBT0219   SBT0220

SBT0221   SBT0222   SBT0223   SBT0224   SBT0225   SBT0226   SBT0227   SBT0228

SBT0232   SBT0233   SBT0234   SBT0235   SBT0236   SBT0237   SBT0238   SBT0239

SBT0240   SBT0241   SBT0242   SBT0243   SBT0244   SBT0245   SBT0246   SBT0247

SBT0248   SBT0249   SBT0250   SBT0251   SBT0252   SBT0253   SBT0254   SBT0255

SBT0256   SBT0257   SBT0258   SBT0259   SBT0260   SBT0261   SBT0262   SBT0263

SBT0264   SBT0265   SBT0266   SBT0267   SBT0272   SBT0273   SBT0274   SBT0275

SBT0276   SBT0277   SBT0278   SBT0279   SBT0280   SBT0281   SBT0282   SBT0283

SBT0284   SBT0285   SBT0286   SBT0287   SBT0288   SBT0289   SBT0290   SBT0291

SBT0292   SBT0293   SBT0294   SBT0295   SBT0296   SBT0297   SBT0298   SBT0299

SBT0300   SBT0301   SBT0302   SBT0303   SBT0304   SBT0305   SBT0306   SBT0307

SBT0308   SBT0309   SBT0310   SBT0311   SBT0312   SBT0313   SBT0314   SBT0315

SBT0316   SBT0317   SBT0328   SBT0329   SBT0330   SBT0331   SBT0332   SBT0333

 SBT0334

SBT0335

SBT0336

SBT0337

SBT0338

SBT0339

SBT0340

SBT0341

 SBT0342

SBT0343

SBT0344

SBT0345

SBT0346

SBT0347

SBT0348

SBT0349

 SBT0351

 SBT0352

SBT0353

 SBT0354

SBT0359

SBT0360

SBT0361

SBT0362

 SBT0363

 SBT0364

SBT0365

 SBT0366

 SBT0367

SBT0368

 SBT0369

 SBT0370

SBT0379

SBT0380

SBT0381

SBT0382

SBT0383

SBT0384

SBT0385

SBT0386

 SBT0387

 SBT0388

 SBT0389

 SBT0390

SBT0391

SBT0392

 SBT0393

SBT0394

 SBT0395

 SBT0396

SBT0397

 SBT0398

SBT0407

SBT0408

 SBT0409

 SBT0410

 SBT0411

 SBT0412

 SBT0413

 SBT0414

SBT0415

 SBT0416

SBT0417

 SBT0418

 SBT0419

 SBT0420

 SBT0421

 SBT0422

 SBT0423

 SBT0424

 SBT0425

 SBT0430

SBT0431

 SBT0432

 SBT0433

 SBT0438

 SBT0439

 SBT0440

 SBT0441

 SBT0442

 SBT0443

SBT0444

SBT0445

SBT0446

SBT0447

SBT0448

SBT0449

SBT0450

 SBT0451

 SBT0452

 SBT0453

 SBT0454

 SBT0455

 SBT0456

 SBT0457

 SBT0458

SBT0459

 SBT0460

 SBT0461

 SBT0462

 SBT0463

 SBT0464

 SBT0465

 SBT0466

 SBT0467

 SBT0468

 SBT0469

SBT0470

 SBT0471

 SBT0472

 SBT0473

 SBT0474

 SBT0475

 SBT0476

 SBT0477

 SBT0478

 SBT0479

 SBT0480

 SBT0481

 SBT0482

 SBT0483

 SBT0484

 SBT0485

 SBT0486

 SBT0487

 SBT0488

 SBT0489

 SBT0490

 SBT0491

 SBT0492

 SBT0493

 SBT0494

 SBT0495

 SBT0496

 SBT0497

 SBT0498

 SBT0499

 SBT0500

 SBT0501

 SBT0502

 SBT0503

 SBT0504

 SBT0505

 SBT0506

  SBT0507

 SBT0508

 SBT0509

 SBT0510

 SBT0511

 SBT0512

 SBT0513

 SBT0514

 SBT0515

 SBT0516

 SBT0517

 SBT0518

 SBT0519

 SBT0520

 SBT0521

SBT0522

SBT0523

SBT0524

SBT0525

SBT0526

SBT0527

SBT0528

SBT0529

SBT0530

SBT0531   SBT0532   SBT0533   SBT0534   SBT0535   SBT0536   SBT0537   SBT0538

SBT0539   SBT0540   SBT0541   SBT0542   SBT0543   SBT0544   SBT0545   SBT0546

SBT0547   SBT0548   SBT0549   SBT0550   SBT0551   SBT0552   SBT0553   SBT0554

SBT0555   SBT0556   SBT0557   SBT0558   SBT0559   SBT0560   SBT0561   SBT0562

SBT0563   SBT0564   SBT0565   SBT0566   SBT0567   SBT0568   SBT0569   SBT0570

SBT0571   SBT0572   SBT0573   SBT0574   SBT0575   SBT0576   SBT0577   SBT0578

SBT0579   SBT0580   SBT0581   SBT0582   SBT0583   SBT0584   SBT0585   SBT0586

 SBT0587

SBT0588

SBT0589

SBT0590

SBT0591

SBT0592

SBT0593

 SBT0594

SBT0595

SBT0596

SBT0597

 SBT0598

 SBT0599

 SBT0600

 SBT0601

SBT0602

SBT0603

 SBT0604

 SBT0605

 SBT0606

 SBT0607

 SBT0608

 SBT0609

 SBT0610

 SBT0611

 SBT0612

 SBT0613

 SBT0614

 SBT0615

 SBT0616

 SBT0617

 SBT0618

SBT0619

 SBT0620

 SBT0621

 SBT0622

 SBT0623

 SBT0624

SBT0625

SBT0626

SBT0627

SBT0628

SBT0629

SBT0630

 SBT0631

 SBT0632

 SBT0633

 SBT0634

 SBT0635

 SBT0636

 SBT0637

 SBT0638

 SBT0639

 SBT0640

 SBT0641

SBT0642

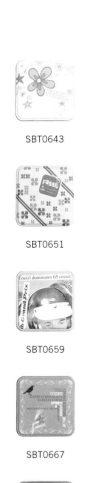      

SBT0643	SBT0644	SBT0645	SBT0646	SBT0647	SBT0648	SBT0649	SBT0650

SBT0651	SBT0652	SBT0653	SBT0654	SBT0655	SBT0656	SBT0657	SBT0658

SBT0659	SBT0660	SBT0661	SBT0662	SBT0663	SBT0664	SBT0665	SBT0666

SBT0667	SBT0668	SBT0669	SBT0670	SBT0671	SBT0672	SBT0673	SBT0674

SBT0675	SBT0676	SBT0677	SBT0678	SBT0679	SBT0680	SBT0681	SBT0682

SBT0683	SBT0684	SBT0685	SBT0686	SBT0687	SBT0688	SBT0689	SBT0690

SBT0691	SBT0692	SBT0693	SBT0694	SBT0695	SBT0696	SBT0697	SBT0698

SBT0699   SBT0700   SBT0701   SBT0702   SBT0703   SBT0704   SBT0705   SBT0706

SBT0707   SBT0708   SBT0709   SBT0710   SBT0711   SBT0712   SBT0713   SBT0714

SBT0715   SBT0716   SBT0717   SBT0718   SBT0719   SBT0720   SBT0721   SBT0722

SBT0723   SBT0724   SBT0725   SBT0726   SBT0727   SBT0728   SBT0729   SBT0730

SBT0731   SBT0732   SBT0733   SBT0734   SBT0735   SBT0736   SBT0737   SBT0738

SBT0739   SBT0740   SBT0741   SBT0742   SBT0743   SBT0744   SBT0745   SBT0746

SBT0747   SBT0748   SBT0749   SBT0750   SBT0751   SBT0752   SBT0753   SBT0754

SBT0755 SBT0756 SBT0757 SBT0758 SBT0759 SBT0760 SBT0761 SBT0762

SBT0763 SBT0764 SBT0765 SBT0766 SBT0767 SBT0768 SBT0769 SBT0770

SBT0771 SBT0772 SBT0773 SBT0774 SBT0775 SBT0776 SBT0777 SBT0778

SBT0779 SBT0780 SBT0781 SBT0782 SBT0783 SBT0784 SBT0785 SBT0786

SBT0787 SBT0788 SBT0789 SBT0790 SBT0791 SBT0792 SBT0793 SBT0794

SBT0795 SBT0796 SBT0797 SBT0798 SBT0799 SBT0800 SBT0801 SBT0802

SBT0803 SBT0804 SBT0805 SBT0806 SBT0807 SBT0808 SBT0809 SBT0810

SBT0811   SBT0812   SBT0813   SBT0814   SBT0815   SBT0816   SBT0817   SBT0818

SBT0819   SBT0820   SBT0821   SBT0822   SBT0823   SBT0824   SBT0825   SBT0826

SBT0827   SBT0828   SBT0829   SBT0830   SBT0831   SBT0832   SBT0833   SBT0834

SBT0835   SBT0836   SBT0837   SBT0838   SBT0839   SBT0840

From 1989 until now (2006) Fossil has continued to design and produce these iconic tins to serve the packaging duties for their watches. The previous cataloging is the most complete to date. Fossil recognizes that some series were omitted due to incomplete archives or photo reference. Additionally, over the years, Fossil has packaged an array of other products in the tin format, but that's another book. This book only takes into account the 3 core shapes that have been used for watches over the past 17 years. As this book was being completed additional designs were being sent out for production. So the beat goes on.

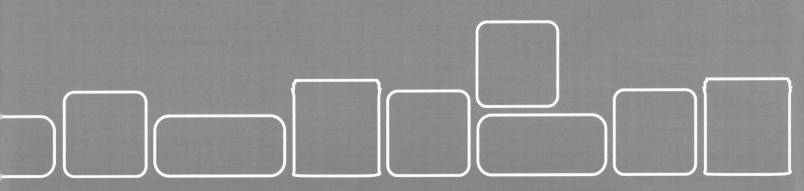

www.fossil.com